DR. RANDY T. JOHNSON

HOPE FOR THOSE
TRAPPED BY LIFE

a
Journey
Back

First Edition, April 2016

Published by:
The River Church
8393 E. Holly Rd.
Holly, MI 48442

Scriptures are taken from the Bible,
English Standard Version (ESV)

Trevor Cole - Cover and Layout

Printed in the United States of America

CONTENTS

5 Introduction

9 Chapter 1: Religion or Relationship

15 Chapter 2: The Dark Veil

19 Chapter 3: The Dark Night of the Soul

25 Chapter 4: The Stanley Cup Picture

31 Chapter 5: A God Send

37 Chapter 6: Friends

43 Chapter 7: Can I Pray for You?

47 Chapter 8: 1 + 1 = 3

51 Chapter 9: A New Man

55 Chapter 10: Bones Wasting Away

61 Chapter 11: Embrace

67 Chapter 12: The Sea Whisperer

71 Chapter 13: Last Words

79 Chapter 14: The Lord Will Provide

85 Chapter 15: "I Will Pray for You"

89 Chapter 16: Favor

93 Chapter 17: Know God, No Fear

97 Chapter 18: Iron Sharpening Iron

105 Chapter 19: My Turn

109 Chapter 20: Curse or Blessing?

115 Chapter 21: Exit Strategy

119 Chapter 22: "I'm Not the Man I Used to Be"

129 Chapter 23: Honest Prayer

133 Chapter 24: Good News

141 Chapter 25: Home Sweet Home

147 Epilogue

INTRODUCTION

March 20, 2000, was the most difficult day of my life.

March 20th is the first day of spring. After a Michigan winter, it is exciting to see plants resurface, greenery fill the trees, and sounds of life and excitement come from the birds who have returned from the south. It is a time where life rises again.

Spring of 2000 was different that year. It was a Monday morning. I was teaching Bible at a Christian school. I didn't have a first-hour class, and the Superintendent had called me to the library. A friend of mine was being convicted of a crime and was scheduled for court that Wednesday. I hadn't seen him much since college. I moved away to Texas for graduate studies and then took a pastorate. We hadn't kept in touch, but we were the kind of friends who could see each other for the first time in five years and not miss a beat. I planned on going to his court date.

I drudged through my classes and then attended golf practice with my team. We were hitting balls in a dome when one of the workers told me I had a call. I needed to get home. My parents were on vacation in Florida, and something went wrong. When I got home, I found out my mom had suddenly passed away.

INTRODUCTION

That spring day I didn't see color, hear the excitement, or feel life in the air. My friend's dreams and goals were dying, and my mom had literally died.

Although I didn't get to stand with my friend in court, over those next three years we got reconnected. I got to share his journey. It has changed me.

In this book, *A Journey Back*, I want to share his real life experiences and show how one can go from the pits of despair to a life of hope and meaning.

The *italicized* sections are his actual thoughts and words.

I trust through this book, those who are in prison and even those who are "free" but trapped by life, will find the hope, value, purpose, and meaning that can only come through the Lord Jesus Christ.

I would like to start by stating that in no way am I attempting to justify or minimize the depth and breadth of my sin and crime. I fell into a state of self-absorbing behavior that harmed and devastated many people that I cared about and loved deeply. At that time, I obviously fell into a state of sin that consumed my reasonable thought process. I didn't concern myself with the welfare of others or the consequences that would take place in many lives, including my own. This book is simply to convey the depth of God's grace that I experienced through dire consequences that resulted from my sin and failure. God disciplined me, and in that consuming fire, I, and hopefully many others, was and will be able to experience His grace, love, and mercy that followed after my conviction and imprisonment. I spent three years in a State prison separated from my family and friends.

I also want to iterate that I am in no way writing this for anyone's pity or concern, as I truly "got what I deserved." Yet, I experienced God's grace in a powerful and personal way. I am not going to go into detail of my sin and crime as I believe that the best focus for the sake of this manuscript is to fix our eyes on what God accomplished in spite of my failures. I was part of a good church, serving in a vibrant and meaningful way until I committed sins against people and God. I was confronted by the Pastors and church board and admitted my sin, although, at that time didn't really take full ownership of my sin and shortcomings. I wrote a letter of repentance and offered to be placed before the entire church for confession and discipline. In my self-centeredness, I was expecting the church to accept me back into the fold with disciplinary action and specific guidelines to be "restored" at a later date. Instead, while I read my letter in front of the church, someone asked my wife to go and get the car and pull it up to an obscure exit to the church. I was escorted into the back tunnel of the church, gently pushed out the door into the rain, and the door was shut behind me. I stood in the rain until my wife pulled up and proceeded to get into the car. I had no further contact with the church as an organization. I will say that some members of the church attempted to reach out to me and offer employment or simply support my family and me, but I was very detached and disillusioned, as I will explain in the first chapter.

INTRODUCTION

RELIGION OR RELATIONSHIP

Church was my main link to God.

I *realized that my relationship with God was not based on a true friendship with Him, but was this diluted relationship that I had established with His church. I was not focused on knowing God on a personal level; I knew the church on that level. I had allowed the church in many ways to truly become my god. The result of that gross misunderstanding of God and His church resulted in my disillusionment with God and disillusionment with the church. Being escorted out into the rain, because of my misguided experience with church, I felt as though God Himself pushed me out of His world and into a "rainy" darkness. Because my concept of relationship was with the church, when the church rejected me, I took that as God's final rejection. This showed me that I was no longer acceptable to Him and certainly not going to be allowed back into His family. I had mistakenly placed the church in the "center" of my walk with "god", and had taken my eyes fully off Jesus. I was truly convinced that God was completely done with me and I had no chance of being in a relationship with Him again. Unfortunately, at that time, I was more devastated that I was out of the church than out of fellowship with God (because I didn't know the difference in my darkened state). Either way, it launched me into a gloominess that I had never experienced before. I had come to Christ at the age of six and had known fellowship with God (perhaps more with the church) my entire memory. The days and months passed as I was going through the court process to determine my future. I had blocked out any chance that God would help me or had any interest in me because of the depth of my sin. I was getting no help from the church, and He, in my*

I was convinced God was completely done with me.

---

opinion at the time, had utterly abandoned me with good cause. I was not angry with Him or bitter with this reality. I simply resigned to the truth that I deserved it and that God "hated" me and was rightfully doing so because of my sin. I was convicted and sentenced to three to fifteen years. I was hanging on to only one hope before my conviction, which was that my attorney may be good enough to keep me home. That was not the case.

Do you have religion or a relationship? _____

_____

_____

The church was designed and instituted by God. We need to be involved in a Christ-centered, Bible-believing Church. However, God wants more. He wants a personal friendship with us. Jesus came to earth to die on the cross for individuals, you and me. He died personally for us. The Church can't save us. The Church doesn't control our destiny.

John 3:16 makes it clear that there are two destinies, "For God so loved the world, that he gave his only Son, that whoever believes in him should not perish but have eternal life." To perish means

Hell and ultimately the Lake of Fire. John points out that although we think eternally, God is interested in spending time with us daily. "Jesus answered him, 'If anyone loves me, he will

For God so loved the world.

keep my word, and my Father will love him, and we will come to him and make our home with him'" (John 14:23). John even goes on to describe this relationship with God as family, "But to all who did receive him, who believed in his name, he gave the right to become children of God" (John 1:12). It is amazing that the God of all creation loves us. He knows us. He wants to spend time with us.

God believes in the Church. He refers to it as His body. However, it cannot replace loyalty and a daily walk with Him.

_____

_____

_____

_____

_____

_____

_____

_____

_____

Throughout his time in prison, I wrote my
friend regularly. He saved 29 of the cards I
sent him. He said other inmates found great
value in them for their lives. Some of them are
included in this book.

*You will never be in a place
where the river
of God's loving kindness
cannot reach you.
The waters of His love
will find their way
into your wilderness...
The streams of His goodness
will flow into
your desert place...
The refreshing of His Spirit
will turn every trial
into a place of praise.*

Roy Lessin

God Will Make A Way!

This card (as the rest) is one I picked out as a reminder of what you already know. All here is cool. I hope and pray you are surviving and thriving.

Your friend,

13

RELIGION OR RELATIONSHIP

2

THE DARK VEIL

I was convinced that God locked me up and threw away the key.

I was placed in a holding cell awaiting transport to the county jail. A dark veil had consumed me with numbness and complete apathy. I had given up any hope. I was convinced that my family would grow to hate me and fear me. I was convinced that God not only locked me away, but also ensured that I would be separated from family, friends, and Him for the rest of my life. The darkness was overwhelming and utterly complete. My life as I knew it was gone for good. I was escorted to the county jail and placed in a holding cell with dozens of men, with no room to move. I was there for several hours trying to avoid any contact with anyone, and the craziness in that room was deafening. Yet, I was in such a dark state I was numb to it all and didn't get phased by any of the behavior. I simply sat there in a trance, knowing that my life was subject to this forever. A guard announced my name and stated that I have a "house" to go to. I ended up in a cell built for six with 11 men. It consisted of six bunks, five "boats" with mattresses, a toilet, shower, and 24-hour lock down. I sat there in the "boat" in my numbed state staring at blank walls and tuning out the arguments, discussions, and fights. I was pulled aside by a guard at one point to describe a fight that took place, and I could

*honestly say that I had no idea that a fight even occurred, even
though it happened less than ten feet from me. I hadn't spoken to
anyone for the couple days I was there. The guy in the bunk next to
my "boat" asked me to teach him from the Bible, as I must know a*

My life as I knew it was gone for good.

---

*lot about it. I hadn't spoken to him, and I didn't even know there
were Bibles in the cell. He handed me an extra Bible and started
asking me questions. I academically answered his questions with
no passion or ownership, as I knew that I wasn't worthy to speak
and certainly not worthy to teach anything from the Bible. From
that day in the county jail, I read the Bible completely through from
front to back and started again until I was shipped out to the State
quarantine facility. I must admit that I didn't learn anything or
gain anything new from reading the Bible. I was still in utter
darkness and despair. My wife had visited me in the county and
all I could do was shed tears and apologize for what I had done to
her and our children.*

Do you feel like God has locked you up and thrown away the key?

_____

_____

Do you feel numb? _____

_____

_____

Have you seen the "dark veil"? _____

_____

_____

The dark veil can come in many forms. It can be the feeling of failure. We get fired, demoted, or overlooked for a promotion. We might have been kicked out of school, declined acceptance to a University, or grades we don't want to discuss. It can be heart-wrenching through relationships such as breaking up, divorce, or children who don't want you to be part of their life. It can come in the form of sorrow in losing one way too early. It can be sin.

Jesus is the light of the world.

The most powerful thing the dark veil does is block the light. Going to the Bible is wise. Reading the Bible even when you don't feel you are getting anything can still be beneficial. However, the only light is Jesus. John 8:12 records, "Again Jesus spoke to them, saying, 'I am the light of the world. Whoever follows me will not walk in darkness, but will have the light of life.'" Jesus is the Light of the World. When Jesus died on the cross, the veil in the temple separating man from God "was torn in two, from top to bottom" (Matthew 27:51). The veil was intimidation. It represented how our sin blocked us from a Holy God. Only the High Priest could go behind the veil and only once a year. Man could not clear the veil separating man from God. Only God could remove it. He tore it from top to bottom. The dark veil has been torn. We can enter the presence of God.

Look for the Light.

THE DARK VEIL

3

THE DARK NIGHT OF THE SOUL

*A*fter two weeks in the County Jail, I was shipped off to the "Quarantine" facility for long-term prisoners. This place made prison a reality. It was exactly how you pictured prison to be from the movies. Every direction I looked, there was cell after cell and gallery after gallery. The noise was so deafening but totally indistinguishable. It was simply noise. I was placed in a small cell with my own toilet and the bars shut with a clank. I was issued clothes and toiletries. I just sat there on the bed in complete numbness and despair for what seemed like hours. It sunk in for the first time that I would not see the light of day for the rest of my life. The spiritual enemy was having a field day with my mind and my thoughts. John of the Cross wrote, "The Dark

---

My soul was dried out and shriveled.

Night of the Soul", and I was fully integrated into my own version of a dark night. My soul was dried out and shriveled into arid dust with absolutely no hope and no purpose at all. A guard came by that looked exactly like James Brown and saw me sitting there. He stated that I needed to make my bed and get dressed because I was going to have an orientation in the chow hall shortly. He said something that should have been encouraging, but I wasn't capable *of hearing it or even processing it. My cell opened 20 minutes later. I had dressed, made up the bed, and shuffled down to the chow hall to see how the rest of my life was about to unfold. It was not going to be very glamorous.*

Two days later, I heard my number over the loudspeaker and was told to pack my stuff. I walked down through the center and another inmate informed me that I was being placed in the pole barns. That didn't sound all that great to me, but he told me that it would be better; I didn't believe him. It was a bit better but didn't fill any part of my darkened soul. A book cart came by every day, and I literally read a paperback novel every day. At first I was selective, then it turned into whatever I was handed I was reading. I can honestly tell you that I probably read 15 books in fifteen days and don't remember anything about any of them. The yard time was at 10:00 am. I was unable to speak to my children from the phones in the yard during the week. I volunteered to work as a bathroom porter because the porters were given an extra fifteen minutes in the yard at night. My children were in school during the day, so I thought this would be an opportunity to call them from the phones at night. I worked three days in the bathrooms before they would let me go outside at night. The first night I was able to go out, I went to the phones to call, and I was informed that we couldn't use the phones during night yard. I made up a reason to quit the bathroom job the next morning. One morning I was given a pass to go to the "classification" building. I sat down in front of the officer and all my paperwork stated that I would be sent to a level one facility. The officer simply looked at me and then again at the paperwork. He crossed out all the "ones" and wrote "twos." He looked at me and stated that he was changing it. I asked why, and what was his reasoning. He stated, "I'm not actually sure, I think you'll see when you get there." God was already moving in miraculous ways on my behalf; I wasn't aware of it and certainly not expecting it. It simply felt like one more nail in the coffin of despair and separation.

Do you know what it feels like when your soul is dried out and shriveled? _____

_____

_____

Do you feel absolutely no hope and no purpose at all?

_____

_____

God is offering hope.

God has a plan. In Genesis 39-41, we read about a man named Joseph who was wrongly accused and thrown in prison. He was innocent. After being in prison for a while, he has a spark of hope as he might get a meeting with the king, basically the parole board. It doesn't happen and chapter 41 starts out "After two whole years." Two years can feel like forever. Be it losing your home, fighting cancer, looking for a job, or waiting for a loved one to finish their tour of duty; two years is long. Joseph's story ends well. He is released, blessed, and able to be a blessing to many more.

Jeremiah 29:11 powerfully says, "For I know the plans I have for you, declares the Lord, plans for welfare and not for evil, to give you a future and a hope." You are more important to God than you probably can ever note. God is offering hope. When your soul is dried up, remember God has a plan and is offering hope.

Proverbs 3:5-6 says, "Trust in the Lord with all your heart, and do not lean on your own understanding. In all your ways acknowledge him, and he will make straight your paths." We need to trust God. We need to seek His direction.

_____

_____

_____

_____

_____

_____

_____

_____

Hey Bud,

Just thinking about you. I hope your thanksgiving was nice. I always wonder if I am off the wall when I think this or ask, because I don't know if any day can be different for you and your schedule. Knowledge can lead to sensitivity. I want you to know I care. Things here are about the same. God is active. Yesterday was the national Day of Reconciliation (Reconciliation, forgiveness, unity & charity). Awesome! Yesterday you could pray in the Senate or the House of Rep, but not in the public school.?! Hopefully, we are on the verge of this changing. I pray that God will continue to bless President Bush and that our president will seek wisdom from God. I shared yesterday with the student body that forgiveness is the aroma flowers put out when they are trampled. It is good to examine what "odor" we put out when we are stepped on. Hopefully, a sweet smelling fragrance to God. I hope you could follow my rambling today!? Your friend,

THE DARK NIGHT OF THE SOUL

4

STANLEY CUP PICTURE

*M*y wife had sent me some pictures of our family and our children to try to cheer me up. Of course, this worked opposite, because, in my darkness, it was a reminder of what I had lost. I put the pictures up on the bulletin board next to my bunk in the pole barns. I was told by several of the inmates and verified by several guards that if you are told you are "riding out" from quarantine at night, it means that you are going to the State facility that is at least 13 hours away from my family. One night around 9 pm, the guard looked over my half wall and said, "Pack up your stuff and bring it to my desk and I'll inventory it, you're riding out." I was in the county jail for 12 days and in quarantine for 24 days. I had not uttered one word to God in that entire time. I felt that I was not worthy to speak to Him. When that guard told me I was "riding out" and it was 9 pm, meaning that I would be as far away from my family as possible, I looked up into heaven and simply stated two words, "It figures!" I still was not blaming God for my consequences or at all angry with Him. I was simply beaten and broken with no glimmer of hope. I packed up my stuff, which wasn't much, and placed it all into a black garbage bag and brought it up to the guard's desk. He dumped it out onto the floor and started documenting everything that was in there on an official form. He got to the pictures of my family, and one of *them was all of us standing with the Stanley Cup after our team had won it. He looked at me and stated that I have an awesome looking family. I may have said thanks, but I'm not sure. He then asked me what I was doing in a place like this. I simply told him*

I was "deservingly wasting time."

---

that I was "deservingly wasting time." He finished inventorying all my stuff and placed it back into the bag and handed it to me. I looked at him with a puzzled look and he informed me that I could go back to my bunk and go to bed; I wasn't "riding out" until the morning. I said I thought if you packed at night you were heading to the facility far away. He looked at me, and said, "Hey, where do you live? I'm not supposed to do this but you seem like a decent guy." I told him, and he said, "You didn't hear this from me, but you are going to the closest place to your family as possible." As I was walking back to my bunk, I said the second thing to God in a month and a half - "Thanks."

Sometimes it is helpful to realize that even some of the great people in the Bible experienced that shriveled, dried up soul.

Peter denied the Lord in Luke 22 three times and actually saw Jesus' face after his denial. This put Peter into a deep darkness and depression knowing that he had failed his Lord and had sinned in a way that Jesus had predicted. Peter's soul was in a darkened, dried up state. In Mark 16, the women encounter a "young man" wearing white and he tells them that Jesus is not in the tomb any longer. He charges the women to, "...go, tell His disciples and Peter..." (Mark 16:7). When this news was brought to the room where the disciples were in fear of the leaders, you can picture Peter sitting in a corner in despair, knowing that he had failed his Lord in the most profound way possible. The women announced that Jesus had risen. They were told to go and tell His disciples and Peter. Peter's name was singled out. This was a moment in Peter's restoration, the beginning of the possibility that God was not done with him, but He had something more for him. It was as if God had reached down from heaven and taken a small eyedropper filled with living water and dropped a small portion on Peter's soul to give it a little life.

I felt that same hope when the guard told me that I was going to be as close to my family as possible. God had taken a portion of

Peter's name was singled out.

His grace and applied it to my soul and given me just a hint of hope. That was the first experience that I had with God in several months after a long drought of lifeless existence. Again, it brought me to a simple, yet very profound place that allowed me to gaze into heaven and say "thanks." My soul, once again, had a tiny droplet of life. The next day I rode out to a prison destination that was, unknowing to me, prepared in advance for my arrival in miraculous ways that are inexplicable.

Look to see what God is doing around you and for you. Take a moment and say, "Thanks."

_____

_____

_____

_____

_____

_____

_____

_____

_____

It was awesome seeing you and a special treat to get and see you and *your wife*. Time flew! Our conversation was so fruitful.

This last weekend I went to our church family camp. We had 90 youth - it went great. I did a workshop. I had the kids (20 at a time) draw a picture of someone who has really hurt them (ie "enemy"). This could be a relative. We then put the pictures on a target and

I had them threw darts at their pictures. It was interesting to watch their emotions. when everyone had at least one turn they sat down. I peeled the target down and had

I believe in you.

a "torn" picture of Jesus underneath. What we do to others - we do to Jesus. powerful object lesson - good response.

Mike, I am still praying and ready for less than 2 months! WOW!

Love ya bro',

Randy

STANLEY CUP PICTURE

5

A GOD SEND

*T*he next morning, I was packed up and placed on a large bus that was very cramped, very crowded, and loud. We spent the entire day traveling around the state dropping men off at various locations. I arrived at my destination around 5 pm, very hungry and again, still very numb. We were brought into a holding room, and the guard was extremely polite and accommodating. He found out that they hadn't fed us all day, and he immediately made arrangements for us to go to the chow hall to eat before we were even processed. The chow hall was very crowded and quite the madhouse. There were two lines and I proceeded to the line that was incredibly long. I got my food and found that

---

He asked if he could pray for me.

---

there was only one seat available on the entire side. I sat down with my food, and a very pleasant man who looked like he was someone's amazing grandpa said hello to me and asked me if he could pray for me, my family, and food. In my numbed and listless state, I simply said, "sure." He proceeded to take my hand and offer up an amazing and loving prayer that encompassed my plight, my family, and my future time in that place. This revealed that he

not only loved God but also had a very intimate relationship with
Him. Even in my state of mind, I remember being impacted by this
man and his wonderful prayer for my family. I ate in silence and
was brought back into the processing room to be transferred to one
of the units.

Is it possible God has sent someone to encourage you during your
time of darkness? _____

_____

_____

Acts 8 records a story about an angel telling Philip, a preacher, to
go to a certain location and meet a man. Verse 27 starts off, "And

---

It is amazing how God can save someone in such a quick instance.

---

he rose and went." Philip met an Ethiopian court official seated
in a chariot reading from Isaiah 29. "And the Spirit said to Philip,
'Go over and join this chariot.' So Philip ran to him and heard him
reading Isaiah the prophet and asked, 'Do you understand what
you are reading?' And he said, 'How can I, unless someone guides
me?' And he invited Philip to come up and sit with him" (Acts
8:29-31). Philip explained the passage sharing the good news of
Jesus. The man accepted the passage and immediately asked to
be baptized. It is amazing how God can save someone in such a
quick instance.

Most messages focus or center around Philip's immediate
obedience on going where he was told to go. This is impressive
and convicts many of us, but maybe we need to see the story from
the one on the receiving end.

This official is reading Isaiah and possibly feeling empty, as he can't understand it. He has a privileged life, yet is needy. A foreigner shows up and can explain the passage. It is life changing. It brings hope.

Look around. Has God placed someone around you that will help you see the light and experience hope? _____

_____

_____

Are you in a readied position to be the person God sends to help others? _____

_____

_____

_____

_____

_____

_____

_____

_____

Hey bud,

I am teaching on Psalm 10
and Psalm 73 tonight. Psalm 10:4
speaks of the wicked... "in all
his thoughts there is no room
for God." What a horrible
picture. v17 points out that
God does hear, He encourages
us and He does listen.
God is good!

In Psalm 73:23
"Yet I am always with you;
you hold me by my
right hand."

*You're in my heart
and prayers.*

So awesome to let God
comfort us, guide us,
and to just take a
walk with Him.

Love ya bro!

I am praying.

A GOD SEND

6

FRIENDS

I *was assigned to a unit, which consisted of two wings and two floors on each wing. I walked up to my wing to enter my room with all the "stuff" that was assigned to me. This is a moment for every inmate to be announced as a newcomer or "fish." I was walking down the sterile looking hallway that consisted of several doors on each side that had a lock and key. A man was staring at me from his open cell door, looking particularly interested in me and gave me a slight nod and smile. This seemed a bit odd, and I wasn't sure how to take the attention. I continued down the hallway and found my cell about four down from his. Later in the first week, he approached me and asked if I would like some company to go to the chow hall. He asked me about myself and offered me a pair of extra sweatpants to wear out in the yard, as the issued pants weren't very comfortable for the yard. I talked to my "Bunkie" about this man and he said that he was one of the coolest guys in the place. I didn't have to worry about him. I had another man ask me in the yard if I was new, and if so, did I come from quarantine. I said yes, and he asked me if I had any of the Johnson's baby lotion, the one in the pink bottle that you can get in quarantine. I laughed and said, "as a matter of fact, yes." He offered me ten times the value of the bottle, but I just gave it to him, as I wasn't going to use it. I tell you this because it turns out the worst things that were happening to me in this prison were very casual and very average events. God was looking after me and protecting me from any craziness. He was placing a hedge around my life even then. I, of course, was very clueless and unaware of this until much later. I later heard stories of what happens to*

God was looking after me.

new guys in prison, and God was literally shielding me from any of that and literally anything at all. Mark, from four doors down, and I struck up a friendship and were soon inseparable. He was a new Christian on a mission looking for God's truth. He asked me several times what denomination I was, and I simply stated that I was a Christian, not quite sure where I was in current standing with God and His church. Mark was soon going to be one of the most dynamic people that God was using to bring me back into fellowship with Him, and in "right/proper" standing with His Church. He had an amazing handle on how to balance church and God!

Life transitions are pivotal in our life. Who we hang out with will determine who we become. This is true in prison, but also for the playground, the college campus, health club, and business world.

Proverbs 13:20 says, "Whoever walks with the wise becomes wise, but the companion of fools will suffer harm." It sounds like guilty

"Iron sharpens iron, and one man sharpens another."

by association, but it is more than that. Often we let the people around us set our measuring standard. We need friends who will challenge us, even when it hurts. Proverbs 27:17 gives an object lesson of this: "Iron sharpens iron, and one man sharpens another." This sharpening involves purposeful friction. It is a designed clash. It is the intentional stepping into someone else's life or him or her stepping into ours for growth. It has often been said, "Do not be deceived: 'Bad company ruins good morals'" (1 Corinthians 15:33).

Evaluate your friendships.

Are you more positive and stronger because of your friends?

_____

_____

Are your friends more productive and whole because of you?

_____

_____

The problem is that people love friendship more than their friends. They will do anything for a friend (lie, steal, and cheat) but won't challenge them. They don't want to hurt the friendship. We need to be more concerned with our friends than the relationship. We need to make sure they are on the right track and that they are willing to hold us accountable, too.

Remember, you are who your friends are!

_____

_____

_____

_____

_____

_____

_____

My man you are studying more now than in school :) Thank you for stretching my mind and faith. I reread your letters and save them all over the place for future thoughts. I had not stopped in a long time and appreciated Pentecost. Amazing! Your timing is also Divine with your letter

A merry heart doeth good
like a medicine.

PROVERBS 17:22

ans your Ezekiel 4? message. I just read Bruce Wilkinson's book the Prayer of Jabez (1 Chron 4:9-10) twice and am preparing a sermon

...by someone who cares!

on it for the chinese adults this Sunday. I am realizing more and more the need for God to work through me in great ways. I have lived on James 1:5 and always ask God to bless me — with wisdom. Yet,

He wants to totally bless me so I can make a difference in other lives (correction: so He can make a difference through me) 1 Chron 4:10 says I should pray to be blessed! James 4:2 says I don't have because I ♥ don't ask. Zechariah 4:6 "Not by might nor by power, but by My Spirit, says the LORD God Almighty." (see also 2 Cor 3:5-6)

Thank you for your thoughts - I want to keep growing. You are loved & prayed for! Your brother,

7

CAN I PRAY FOR YOU?

*D*uring this same timeframe (very early in my time in prison), I was sitting at a table in the dayroom reading a novel of some sort. A young man approached me and asked if he could sit down for a moment. He introduced himself and asked my name. I go by my middle name, and gave him that name, as I was not wary of him or anyone at that point. My entire being was still numb and resigned to utter failure and lack of any hint of self-worth. He looked at me with a strange expression and stated that wasn't really my name at all. He then went on to ask

I have been praying for you every day.

if I had been in ministry before. Now, I was getting cautious, this person seemed to know too much about me, and it was making me very uneasy. He went on to describe the day that my case went public, and the news channels aired my story on the 12:00 pm news. He stated that he was in his room for count time, and for no reason at all, turned on the news that day. He also stated that he never turned his TV on during the 12:00 pm count. He was touched by my case and my story that he watched that day, and God laid me on his heart. He looked at me across the table and said, "I knew you were going to end up here, I've been praying for you every day and asking God to restore you and do miraculous things in your recovery." It turned out that this young man was the leader of the church group in the unit that I was assigned. He also led two Bible studies a week in the dayroom of the unit. This was not an acceptable activity for the Department of Corrections, but God had granted His grace and it was never challenged or stopped. God had prepared this man and his prayer for me months in advance for this amazing meeting in a prison dayroom.

Do you have someone you are praying for? _____
_____
_____

Do you know of someone who regularly prays for you?
_____
_____

In Acts chapter 12, Herod has already killed James and had proceeded to arrest Peter. He put Peter in total shut down with four squads of soldiers assigned to him alone. Verse five simply states, "So Peter was kept in prison, but earnest prayer for him was made to God by the church." People were praying for him. The chapter goes on to record the miracle of an angel coming and delivering Peter from Herod and specifically prison. The story continues, "When he realized this, he went to the house of Mary, the mother of John whose other name was Mark, where many were gathered together and were praying. And when he knocked at the door of the gateway, a servant girl named Rhoda came to answer. Recognizing Peter's voice, in her joy she did not open the gate but ran in and reported that Peter was standing at the gate. They said to her, 'You are out of your mind.' But she kept insisting that it was so, and they kept saying, 'It is his angel!' But Peter continued knocking, and when they opened, they saw him and were amazed" (Acts 12:12-16). They were praying and couldn't believe it when their prayer was answered. The key is, they knew prayer was powerful. They knew they needed to pray for Peter. Even if you don't "feel" that your prayers are being heard or answered, keep praying because God promises that they are.

1 Timothy 2:1-3 tells us that we are to pray for others, "First of all, then, I urge that supplications, prayers, intercessions, and thanksgivings be made for all people, for kings and all who are in high positions, that we may lead a peaceful and quiet life, godly and dignified in every way. This is good, and it is pleasing in the sight of God our Savior." We are to pray for all people.

We should pray that people love more.

Philippians 1:9-11 gives us some ideas of what to pray for others, "And it is my prayer that your love may abound more and more, with knowledge and all discernment, so that you may approve what is excellent, and so be pure and blameless for the day of Christ, filled with the fruit of righteousness that comes through Jesus Christ, to the glory and praise of God." We should pray that people love more. Also, we should pray that as they grow in knowledge, they would also have discernment. Finally, we should pray for righteousness; hopefully right choices will bring right actions.

We are to pray for others, but please realize you have been prayed for. After Jesus had spent time praying for His disciples, He prayed for us, "I do not ask for these only, but also for those who will believe in me through their word, that they may all be one, just as you, Father, are in me, and I in you, that they also may be in us, so that the world may believe that you have sent me. The glory that you have given me I have given to them, that they may be one even as we are one, I in them and you in me, that they may become perfectly one, so that the world may know that you sent me and loved them even as you loved me" (John 17:20-23).

Jesus has prayed for you and there may be others, too.

_____

_____

_____

_____

_____

_____

_____

8

1 + 1 = 3

That same week, I was sitting in the dayroom about 15 minutes before we were going to be called to the "chow hall" for lunch. A very short, very stocky boxer type young man named Jay approached me and asked if I knew anything about the Bible. I was baffled and said, "Maybe a little!" He asked me an interesting question about the Old Testament, and we discussed many answers for the brief 15 minutes as we waited for lunch. He thanked me and moved on. This led to a very important transition in my time behind bars. I was still in a very dark place in my soul and still saw very little hope that God had a plan for me again. I was stuck in the depths of depression and emptiness, in constant accusation of myself for being an utter and complete failure with no light in my life. I will skip ahead about a month for this section and will backtrack in chapters to come to share why this encounter had a huge impact on my future life behind bars and out. I finally received a "call out" for church service ("Call out" is an approved request to go to a different building or be involved in a unique activity that requires permission from the Department of Corrections). I attended my first church service, which was in a classroom with about 40 men. The Chaplain came into the room just before the service was about to begin, approached the young man "Jay", and had a focused conversation. I could tell that something was amiss but had no idea what that could be. I watched them in their discussion, and then something very confusing was happening. They were both looking at me and "Jay" was pointing directly at me. The Chaplain made a "beeline" for me and asked me to join her in the back closet. She simply said, "Our volunteer just informed me that they were not going to be here for the service, and I need someone to preach. I hear that you have a background in ministry, or at least, know a

---

This led to a very important transition time in my time behind bars.

---

lot about the Bible from "Brother Jay." Is that true?" I was totally caught off guard and was mortified that she may be asking me to preach in the service in about 10 minutes. I said that I couldn't do that and that I was in no place to preach at all! This amazing Chaplain simply looked at me and said bluntly, "What? You did something wrong, and now you think that God can't use you or you're not qualified to do God's work?" I said, "Yes, that is exactly what I am saying!" She responded, "You are preaching in 10 minutes and I am going to make that announcement the moment I walk out of this room. You can't back out because they will all be counting on you!" I recalled a sermon that I had preached about "Gideon" from the book of Judges and preceded to preach in the church service that I was sure I didn't even belong in. God was beginning to get my attention that He was not done with me and that He still had some plans for my life in prison. I was still convinced that God would have nothing for me outside of prison.

Have you ever felt unworthy to be in Church and especially God's presence? _____

_____

_____

Are you involved in a chapel, church, or gathering of Christians?

_____

_____

Have you ever skipped "Communion" because of sin?

_____

_____

The point of Communion, or the breaking of bread, is to right ourselves with God. It is a time of reflection to determine if there is any sin that is hindering your relationship with our Lord. Don't skip "Communion", utilize its purpose to confess, repent, and get right with God.

Get with others; get with Him.

Being involved with other believers is crucial. Hebrews 10:24-25 says, "And let us consider how to stir up one another to love and good works, not neglecting to meet together, as is the habit of some, but encouraging one another, and all the more as you see the Day drawing near." Chapel, or Church, gives us an opportunity to encourage others and be encouraged. Unfortunately, people get into the habit of not going. Excuses abound, but basically, it is the result of misplaced priorities. We need to make it a priority to be in Church. When we feel we don't need it, we need to be there for others. However, generally, we need it.

Acts 2:42 shows how Church was a priority with the early followers of Jesus, "They were continually devoting themselves to the apostles' teaching and to fellowship, to the breaking of bread and to prayer." They were devoted. It was important. They made it a priority to meet together.

Remember: "For where two or three have gathered together in My name, I am there in their midst" (Matthew 18:20). The last two verses of Matthew are a command from Jesus. He says, "Go therefore and make disciples of all nations, baptizing them in the name of the Father and of the Son and of the Holy Spirit, teaching them to observe all that I have commanded you. And behold, I am with you always, to the end of the age" (Matthew 28:19-20). He tells us to go and make disciples (emphasizing evangelism and reaching others), baptize and observe items He commanded (emphasizing Church and gathering together), and teach (emphasizing that every believer needs to grow). Last words tend to hold more significance, value, and meaning. We need to obey. We need to get together with other believers. We all have something to give.

_____

_____

_____

_____

_____

_____

_____

_____

9

A NEW MAN

I must say that sometimes in life, you meet someone that is of such high quality of character, that you can't avoid them. I was drawn to Mark immediately, in such a profound way that I can't begin to describe the depth of our friendship in writing. Mark was and is one of the most important people that I have ever encountered in my entire life. We began spending time together in the yard and in the dayrooms just talking about life, God, and getting to know each other. This instantly became a lifelong friendship. "Friendship is unnecessary, like philosophy, like art... It has no survival value; rather it is one of those things that give value to survival" (C.S. Lewis). Mark would challenge me every day with thoughts from the Bible and general insights that he was developing. He would read his Bible every night and keep a yellow legal pad next to him to jot down questions about different passages. I would answer them to the best of my ability, but it usually ended with a two-way conversation working through the answers together. He had a hunger and a thirst for God that I had never seen before. This led to hours each day in discussion, laughter, and friendship. That was the first real thing that was helping me realize that my life was far from "over." Mark and I were on the same wing. Each night when the midnight count was over, we could leave our cells and go to the bathroom. We would *have a Bible and notebook in hand and discuss what we had read. We spent time in the open bathroom praying together. The first night we did this, the third shift Corrections Officer walked by and stopped. He asked us what we were doing, and when we told him, we were both certain that we would be kicked out for violating the rule that we weren't allowed to "gather" after hours. He simply said*

We spent time praying in the open bathroom together.

that we could stay as long as he didn't get any complaints, and we kept the noise down. Something amazing began happening at our late-night Bible studies and prayer vigils. Men started coming in on a nightly basis with specific prayer requests, and we were praying for several men each night in the bathroom. A few weeks of this every night, and we had a following of men asking for prayer. One night, the Corrections Officer that had given us "permission" walked into the bathroom and waited until everyone else left. We apologized and were about to leave also when he stopped us and told us that his wife was going into surgery the next day and asked us to pray for her. He stood about ten feet from us because he couldn't "join" us in prayer but was able to hear Mark and I pray for his wife's surgery, asking God to heal her, and watch over the procedure. The next evening, he came into the bathroom to let us know that his wife's surgery went fine. Then he broke down and through tears of joy told us that the doctors could find no sign of cancer. He gave his life to Jesus that night in a lowly prison bathroom through tears of joy and celebration!

Have you given your life to Jesus? _____

_____

_____

If not, what is holding you back? _____
_____
_____

If you have given your life to Jesus, who has been involved in your journey? _____
_____
_____

It would be interesting to know the Correction Officer's full story. In 1 Corinthians 3 Paul says, "I planted, Apollos watered, but God gave the growth. So neither he who plants nor he who waters is anything, but only God who gives the growth. He who plants and he who waters are one, and each will receive his wages according to his labor. For we are God's fellow workers. You are God's field, God's building" (verses 6-9). Most people don't get saved through a single sermon or encounter with God. It is a journey. It is our responsibility and privilege to help others come to the Lord.

Paul's journey was bold. He studied the Old Testament regularly and even taught it to others. He was anti-Jesus and anti-anyone who was a follower of Jesus. He was so cynical that he had a Christian leader stoned to death. Acts 7 ends, "Then they cast him out of the city and stoned him. And the witnesses laid down their garments at the feet of a young man named Saul. And as they were stoning Stephen, he called out, 'Lord Jesus, receive my spirit.' And falling to his knees he cried out with a loud voice, 'Lord, do not hold this sin against them.' And when he had said this, he fell asleep" (verses 58-60). Chapter 8 starts, "And Saul approved of his execution." Paul's name used to be Saul. When he became of a follower of Jesus, he became a new man and took a new name, Paul.

Saul (Paul) read the Bible. He saw the life and heard the testimony of Stephen. Even death couldn't stop the message. Finally, Jesus personally confronted Saul. Acts 9:1-6 give the

"Therefore if anyone is in Christ, he is a new creation."

details, "But Saul, still breathing threats and murder against the disciples of the Lord, went to the high priest and asked him for letters to the synagogues at Damascus, so that if he found any belonging to the Way, men or women, he might bring them bound to Jerusalem. Now as he went on his way, he approached Damascus, and suddenly a light from heaven shone around him. And falling to the ground he heard a voice saying to him, 'Saul, Saul, why are you persecuting me?' And he said, 'Who are you, Lord?' And he said, 'I am Jesus, whom you are persecuting. 6 But rise and enter the city, and you will be told what you are to do.'" From that point on Saul became a preacher of the good news of Jesus Christ. Saul became Paul.

2 Corinthians 5:17 says, "Therefore, if anyone is in Christ, he is a new creation. The old has passed away; behold, the new has come."

Who are you? _____

_____

_____

_____

_____

_____

_____

_____

10

BONES WASTING AWAY

*O*ne day I was sitting in my cell in the middle of the day, and the phone at the base rang loudly. The time of my crime and my sin had brought me to a place of guilt and shame even before I was "caught", and it was all exposed. I remember very clearly that each time the phone would ring at home, I was in a state of fear and trembling because of all the sin that I was trying to cover up through that terrible time in my life. I was in a constant condition of "cover up" and dread of exposure. I was tortured by the darkness of my own behavior and sin. Back to

I was in constant condition of "cover up" and dread of exposure.

the day when the phone rang at the base, I remember thinking very clearly as if a voice from above said to me that God has shown me amazing grace. The ringtone on that phone was exactly the same ringtone as the one at home. I remember feeling a sense of relief and thankfulness that even though I was incarcerated, I had peace that I no longer had to worry about exposure. God, in His infinite grace and mercy, had exposed my crime and sin and had moved me forward to a place where I could embrace Him and my life once again without any more fear of my past sinful behavior.

Sin can consume us. It can eat away at our very souls.

Do you know the feeling? _____

_____

_____

Bible hero David had quite the journey. Although he defeated a giant and saved a nation, he also committed adultery and murder.

God is offering us forgiveness.

In Psalm 32:3-4 he says, "For when I kept silent, my bones wasted away through my groaning all day long. For day and night your hand was heavy upon me; my strength was dried up as by the heat of summer." He felt like his bones were wasting away. He hid his sin, but it owned him. It physically beat him up. David continues, "For I know my transgressions, and my sin is ever before me" (Psalm 51:3). David woke up thinking about his sin. He thought of his sin throughout the day. He went to sleep regretting his sin. He feared he was living his nightmares. The sin and guilt didn't go away until he confessed it. He again felt free.

He writes in Psalm 32:1-2, "Blessed is the one whose transgression is forgiven, whose sin is covered. Blessed is the man against whom the Lord counts no iniquity, and in whose spirit there is no deceit." A forgiven person becomes refreshed. David experienced forgiveness.

God is offering us forgiveness.

1 John 1:9 promises, "If we confess our sins, he is faithful and just to forgive us our sins and to cleanse us from all unrighteousness."

Hiding our sin is illogical. God knows all. We can't hide. He just wants us to confess our sin and He will wipe us clean. Isaiah 43:25 adds, "I, I am he who blots out your transgressions for my own sake, and I will not remember your sins."

When we confess our sin, God forgives us – every time. Now, we need to be willing to forgive ourselves.

"So if the Son sets you free, you will be free indeed" (John 8:36).

_____

_____

_____

_____

_____

_____

_____

_____

Your letter encouraged me greatly! I know that no matter where we are, every day is a battle to keep positive and overcome Satan's weapon of discouragement. I will pray for growth and a positive mindset. I am thankful that God is watching out for you.

As far as topics to research, I would like your thoughts, cross references illustrations, and applications. Presently, we have been going through the fruit of the Spirit (Galatians 5:22). We have other service projects and programs for December, so we don't get back ~~to~~ to these fruits until January. The last three (faithfulness, gentleness, and self-control) are the only ones left. I would love your thoughts.

May the Lord
bless you,
refresh you,
and meet your
every need.

Your friends,

Randy

BONES WASTING AWAY

11

EMBRACE

*S*hortly after I arrived at the level two prison, my wife and children were set up to visit me on a Sunday afternoon. I received the call from base that I had a visit and got ready with eager anticipation to see my family after the long separation. When they walked into the visiting room, I was surprised to see that it was my sister with my children. I soon learned that my wife was struggling with my sin and the consequences of them. She decided to "think through" whether she wanted to continue in a marriage with someone like me. It was great to see my children, but it was

I was convinced that my wife would come to hate me.

also devastating to hear this news about my wife. The first thing that I thought was that she was completely correct in her choice, as I certainly wasn't worth anything to anyone. Upon my initial incarceration, I remember thinking that I had ruined my life and the lives of my wife and children. I was convinced that my wife would come to hate me and that my children would soon follow in that hatred. This was one of the most compelling thoughts that caused me to slip into a pit of darkness and despair. On that first visit, my children were loving and wonderful, even eager to see *me and spend time with me. That was a delight in a dark life. I spent the next three months writing to my wife with no response, and calling (collect) the house, where she would answer, but when the charges were approved, my children would be on the phone. I didn't have any contact from my wife for about three months' time. At the end of that three month period, my sister was scheduled to visit me with my children, and when I was in the visiting room, the face that I saw enter was my lovely wife. My thoughts were, "this could be really good, or this could be really bad!" We approached each other and she initiated a long, loving hug, and looked up into my eyes through tears and said, "I'm so sorry!" I couldn't believe my ears! I said back to her; "You don't have anything to be sorry about, I'm just glad you are here!" We sat there with tear filled eyes and discussed our future together, plans for the kids, and how things were out in the world for her. God answered my hours of prayer and brought our marriage on the road to recovery and restoration.*

Do you remember some of your broken relationships?

_____

_____

Did any of them ever get restored? _____

_____

_____

How did you feel? _____

_____

_____

Luke 15 records a familiar story: "And he said, "There was a man who had two sons. And the younger of them said to his father, 'Father, give me the share of property that is coming to me.' And he divided his property between them. Not many days later, the younger son gathered all he had and took a journey into a far country, and there he squandered his property in reckless living. And when he had spent everything, a severe famine arose in that country, and he began to be in need. So he went and hired himself out to one of the citizens of that country, who sent him into his fields to feed pigs. And he was longing to be fed with the pods that the pigs ate, and no one gave him anything" (verses 11-16).

One son wanted his inheritance while his dad was still alive. He felt he was entitled to it. He just wanted the money so he could be his own man. In the process, he left his family behind as if they didn't live anymore. He wasted the money. It was gone and he had no one or thing to fall back on. He was at his lowest point. Finally, he decides to humble himself and just see if his father will take him back.

"Draw near to God, and He will draw near to you."

The story continues, "But when he came to himself, he said, 'How many of my father's hired servants have more than enough bread, but I perish here with hunger! I will arise and go to my father, and I will say to him, "Father, I have sinned against heaven and before you. I am no longer worthy to be called your son. Treat me as one of your hired servants."' And he arose and came to his father. But while he was still a long way off, his father saw him and felt compassion, and ran and embraced him and kissed him. And the son said to him, 'Father, I have sinned against heaven and before you. I am no longer worthy to be called your son.' But the father said to his servants, 'Bring quickly the best robe, and put it on

him, and put a ring on his hand, and shoes on his feet. And bring
the fattened calf and kill it, and let us eat and celebrate. For this
my son was dead, and is alive again; he was lost, and is found.'
And they began to celebrate" (Luke 15:17-24).

I can imagine the son. His thoughts are, "I am a worm and not
a man" (Psalm 22:6). He feels horrible. The trip is slow and
his feet don't want to move forward. Each step would ache with
shame. His head is down. His eyes lack life and direction. He
slowly drudges forward. However, look at the Father. He has
been watching in hope and anticipation. The Father ran to him.
They embrace. They celebrate. Their relationship is restored.

Please realize in this parable, the Father is God. He wants a
relationship with you. James 4:8 says, "Draw near to God, and he
will draw near to you." The son started toward the Father, and
the Father ran to him. You might be asking, "How do I draw near
to God? What is my first step?" The second half of James 4:8
says, "Cleanse your hands, you sinners, and purify your hearts,
you double-minded." Confess your sins and change your ways.
God will help. Your relationship with God will be restored. You
get to see God run. Angels are celebrating.

Confusion - I came by one time to visit and the form wasn't there, and then it is another time. Sorry bud, we will try to connect.

          that I loved reading your letter. I like your phrase "perhaps God has something more personal and intimate for my life." I am reading "Experiencing God." I like being reminded that we have a relationship not a religion. Great question you ask: "Are you in a position to hear God's 'still small voice?'" I just finished reading "How to start a revival" by Charles Finney. He lived this - good challenge. Live pure life, seek God, seek souls! I am trying to be more sensitive to the Holy Spirit's urging. My mission field is World's Gym. I am trying to be friendly, be open, get personal, and share Christ. I gave out a Gospel of John and hope to give many more. This is my time for physical and spiritual exercise. God is blessing me and my family. I hope to see you soon. Keep pressing on one step at a time. Love - your friend,

Randy

EMBRACE

12

THE SEA WHISPERER

The "yard" became a very pivotal place for my early recovery and restoration process. The older man that I met at the chow hall on the first day quickly became an important mentor and leader in my ability to see that God had forgiveness available to me. Also, that God still loved me in spite of my sin and short comings. Bob had started a "prayer table" in the yard long before I got there and was available each morning to pray with anyone and everyone that requested. I joined his table every day that I was available, and soon found a confident and powerful way in which to approach God's throne and presence. Dozens of men were joining us each day to ask for prayer about anything and everything in their lives.

Prayer table

Bob would also use that time to share the love of Jesus and to give teaching on God's Word. Bob was an awesome teacher and was filled with the gift of compassion. Each person at the table quickly realized that there was no judgment or condemnation at that table and were confident to share many deep, personal secrets and issues. The inmate church decided to have a basketball game one Saturday to develop community and unity among the different housing units. I had played a lot of basketball in the past and was convinced that this would be a way to bridge any gap that may exist between the other men and me. On the first play of the game, I came down wrong on my knee and it exploded in pain. God quickly showed me that "my way" in the past of "bridging" was not going to be His plan behind bars. It was yet another way in which God had revealed Himself to me, even though it was painful and unpleasant. I was appreciative that he was moving me forward in a different way than I had chosen my whole life before. The "yard" continued to be a peaceful place where God was granting true spiritual growth and dynamic friendships.

Do you ever feel frustrated when things don't go the way you expected? _____

_____

_____

Mark chapter 4 records a time when the disciples, several of them being fishermen, thought they were in their comfort zone only to hit by a storm: "On that day, when evening had come, he said to them, 'Let us go across to the other side.' And leaving the crowd, they took him with them in the boat, just as he was. And other boats were with him. And a great windstorm arose, and the waves were breaking into the boat, so that the boat was already filling. But he was in the stern, asleep on the cushion. And they woke him and said to him, 'Teacher, do you not care that we are perishing?' And he awoke and rebuked the wind and said to the sea, 'Peace! Be still!' And the wind ceased, and there was a great calm. He said to them, 'Why are you so afraid? Have you still no faith?' And they were filled with great fear and said to one another, 'Who then is this, that even the wind and the sea obey him?'" (verses 35-41).

We will be hit by storms. Life will feel out of control. We won't be holding the steering wheel directing the day or possibly even our future. When this happens, we just need to call on Jesus. He controls all of life; "even the wind and the sea obey him".

God establishes your steps.

Isaiah 55:8-9 remind us, "For my thoughts are not your thoughts, neither are your ways my ways, declares the Lord. For as the heavens are higher than the earth, so are my ways higher than your ways and my thoughts than your thoughts." God sees the big picture. He knows, holds, and controls the future. He doesn't get tossed about.

Please remember to do your best knowing, "The heart of man plans his way, but the Lord establishes his steps" (Proverbs 16:9). God establishes your steps. He's got your back. He is never caught off-guard. He is never surprised. He is God, He made you, and He has a plan for you.

_____

_____

_____

_____

_____

_____

_____

_____

_____

13

LAST WORDS

One of the major assets of being locked up is the massive amount of time that you have to accomplish "something". Many inmates spend very little time attempting to better themselves intellectually or spiritually. One of the main things that God was showing me was to utilize the time that I had to spend in His Word, self-reflection, and mostly, getting to know God in an intimate and personal way. God showed me that He was very accessible and willing to interact with me through His Word and intimate time in prayer with the Almighty God. Several times a day I was forced onto my bunk for "count" times. These times would last from 30 minutes to an hour depending on the situation. One day as I was lying on my bunk, I was meditating over God's Word, and I heard the words "Consider Stephen!" I'm pretty sure that the words were not audible as I leaned over and looked at my "bunkie" and he was fast asleep. But they were words that I heard in some fashion in my mind. It didn't make much sense to me as I thought about why I would "consider Stephen", but I knew that God was already doing many things on my behalf. I decided to listen to the still small voice and press on with the consideration of the disciple Stephen from the book of Acts. I systematically went through all the facts that I could think of about Stephen. When I got to the end, when he looked up into heaven and saw

Jesus standing at the right hand of the Father, and then he died, I still didn't receive any stellar epiphany about the man. The last thing that came into my mind was that Saul/Paul was holding the clothing of the men that were stoning Stephen. A light bulb went on that this was God's way of getting me to think about all

---

Locked away was my own "road to redemption and restoration."

---

the terrible things that Saul had done to the Church of Jesus before God brought him to submission and blinded him on the road to Damascus. God revealed to me that this time locked away was my own "road to redemption and restoration." I had been blinded by my own sin and cast into emptiness and brokenness, and it was only then that God could seize my attention and get me to a place of submission and willingness to be consumed by His cleansing fire. I gave myself over to His Master's touch to do anything necessary to bring me into a right relationship with Him. Not His church, not His Word, He made it very clear that I was to focus my attention on "Knowing Him!"

Stephen's life ends in dramatic fashion. As he is being killed, Acts 7:56 records, "And he said, 'Behold, I see the heavens opened, and the Son of Man standing at the right hand of God.'" The passage continues with Stephen's last words. He makes two statements:
1. "Lord Jesus, receive my spirit."
2. "Lord, do not hold this sin against them."

When all is said and done, Stephen wants to be with God. He wants others to experience God's love, too.

What is your desire? _____

Are you investing your time wisely so that you can meet Jesus
with no regrets? _____

_____

_____

Time management is important. When death becomes closer,
most people evaluate how they spent their life. Ephesians 5:15-
17 says, "Look carefully then how you walk, not as unwise but
as wise, making the best use of the time, because the days are
evil. Therefore do not be foolish, but understand what the will
of the Lord is." Time is more valuable than money. When you
spend money, there is the potential to get more. Time has a limit;
once it is spent, it is gone. Spend wisely "making the best use of
the time". Colossians 4:5 repeats the command, "Walk in wisdom
toward outsiders, making the best use of the time."

Psalm 90:12 adds a whole other insight, "So teach us to number
our days that we may get a heart of wisdom." Obviously, inmates
have a countdown until they might get out. However, we tend to
rush life along. We can't wait to get married, then to have a child,
then for them to sleep through the night, walk, talk, go to school,
graduate, get married, and have our grandchildren. Meanwhile,
we are always focused on the next step, promotion, and eventually
retirement. Before we know it, we have wished our life away. We
need to learn how to "number our days." We need to make the
most of each stage of our life.

Don't wait until life is easier or better; focus on knowing God
better now. In Colossians 1:9 Paul's prayer for his people is
expressed: "And so, from the day we heard, we have not ceased to
pray for you, asking that you may be filled with the knowledge of
his will in all spiritual wisdom and understanding." Paul wants
them to be "filled with the knowledge of his will". He wants them

to know God and His plans better. It was even Paul's prayer for himself, "that I may know him and the power of his resurrection" (Philippians 3:10). This was Paul's prayer while he was in prison. He wanted to know God better and didn't wait until he got "out."

Focus on knowing God better now.

That should be our prayer for family, friends, and us. Jesus is straightforward saying, "And this is eternal life, that they know you the only true God, and Jesus Christ whom you have sent" (John 17:3).

Jeremiah 9:23-24 makes knowing God the best thing ever, "Thus says the Lord: 'Let not the wise man boast in his wisdom, let not the mighty man boast in his might, let not the rich man boast in his riches, but let him who boasts boast in this, that he understands and knows me, that I am the Lord who practices steadfast love, justice, and righteousness in the earth. For in these things I delight, declares the Lord.'"

Finally, you might be asking, "how can I know God better?" The obvious answers are the Bible and Church / Chapel, but John gives another step, "Anyone who does not love does not know God, because God is love" (1 John 4:8). Love God and love others – this fulfills all the commandments.

Who should you show more love to? _____

How? _____

When? _____

LAST WORDS

"Love is the doorway through which the human soul passes from selfishness to service." – Jack Hyles

_____

_____

_____

_____

_____

_____

_____

_____

God's light is like the

dawn, brighter than the sun…

May you come

to see what hope you

have in Him,

and how extraordinarily

great the power

that He has exercised

for you…

and be encouraged.

It was so good to see you!! My soul was encouraged. Time flew. I bought Secrets of the Vine to read later this week. Right now I am studying Jonathan Edwards' sinners in the hands of an angry God. "Unconverted men walk over the pit of hell on a rotten covering..." what a great reminder - preach the word! Never minister again - you already are. When you get this card you

May you sense His presence with you today.!

should only have 1 more year.
What a thought - use the time
wisely, the time frame of your
ministry there is winding down.
I look forward to reading
secrets of the vine and the
always needed reminder of
the power of prayer.

Love you Bro,

14

THE LORD WILL PROVIDE

*O*ne evening in our unit, the church group decided to hold a "banquet" for the entire unit for anyone who was hungry and wanted to partake in the "cook up." This included different foods and condiments that were available through the "store" and anyone that was willing donated different food types and the leaders in the church prepared the meal for the unit. It was an amazing time of sharing, fellowship, and introducing men to the love of Christ in a real and intimate way. Hundreds of inmates joined in the celebration, and everyone ate as much as they wanted. It seemed very similar to the feeding of the 5000 when Jesus told His disciples to find food and feed all the people who were hungry. God was not only present in prison, but He was very interested in each person and was available for anyone in need. We just kept on serving food until everyone in line had eaten his fill, and we had some leftover. The Unit Guard told the church

God still had plans for my life and still loved me unconditionally.

leaders that they could bring any leftovers to the school building and feed anyone that wanted to eat over there. God's favor was reaching in many places in that "dark place", and many times the

THE LORD WILL PROVIDE

darkness was destroyed by the incredible light of our Lord and Savior Jesus Christ. It was apparent to me in this early stage of my recovery and incarceration that God was not only present in this place, but He was powerful, mighty, loving, and caring to all who were reaching out to Him. God was revealing Himself to me personally in so many ways that I couldn't ignore the fact that He still had plans for my life and still loved me unconditionally. The amazing truth of God's discipline is that He shines a beacon of love and light in the midst of it! My life was continuing to improve and my soul was being watered and saturated with the love of God, family, old friends reaching out to me through letters and visits, and new friends that I never dreamed I would meet in the dreadfulness of prison.

I can't imagine how much food was necessary to fill so many hungry men. It reminds me of John 6 where Jesus feeds 5,000 men along with a lot of women and children from a single boy's lunch. Another amazing story takes place in 2 Kings 4 when Elisha causes the widow's oil to flow endlessly. Her faith had her asking people all around for empty jars. She was blessed beyond imagination. It is exciting to visit these stories and watch people scratch their heads and just stand there in amazement.

Psalm 23:1 tells us, "The Lord is my shepherd; I shall not want." God loves us and will take care of us. He will meet our needs.

The story of Abraham sacrificing Isaac (Genesis 22) has so much suspense. The journey was already heart wrenching when Isaac notices they have everything but the sacrificial animal. Abraham says, "God will provide." Abraham continues with the process and at the last moment, God steps in. He stops Abraham. God shows the rest of His plan: "And Abraham lifted up his eyes and looked, and behold, behind him was a ram, caught in a thicket by his horns. And Abraham went and took the ram and offered it up as a burnt offering instead of his son." (verse 13). I have never

---

God will provide.

---

seen a ram caught in a thicket. Their instincts and skills don't allow for this. However, on this occasion, it happened. Verse 14 gives Abraham's response, "So Abraham called the name of that place, 'The Lord will provide; as it is said to this day, 'On the mount of the Lord it shall be provided.'" The Lord will provide.

_____
_____
_____
_____
_____
_____
_____
_____
_____

"...GOD SENT HIS ONLY BEGOTTEN SON
INTO THE WORLD,
THAT WE MIGHT LIVE THROUGH HIM."

I JOHN 4:9 KJV

Hey Bud,

thinking about you
and hope that some way
special God will make
this Christmas Fresh

...so that we would have everything we need.

MAY JESUS BE THE
JOY OF YOUR
CHRISTMAS CELEBRATION

Keep the Faith,

Your friend,

[signature]

THE LORD WILL PROVIDE

15

"I WILL PRAY FOR YOU"

O ne day I heard some commotion down on the "base" and came out of my room to see several of the Christian men with smiles and hand slaps greeting my good friend Bob into our unit. This was truly a blessing for me as it would allow me to spend a lot of time with Bob in the day rooms. We were just becoming friends, and I knew this would be a great time of growth for me and many others in our Housing Unit. One afternoon, Bob and I were sitting at a table in the dayroom studying God's Word when he looked at me and stated that he wanted to pray for me. I hadn't revealed anything about my life, past, or sin to Bob as of

It felt as if God was reaching out of heaven and embracing me personally.

that time. We bowed our heads and Bob began the most beautiful, intimate prayer for me that I had ever heard or was a part of. He prayed for specific things that were happening in my life and I was so overwhelmed with joy and peace and knew that God was leading that prayer time. It felt as if God was reaching out of heaven and embracing me personally. Tears were flowing freely as I sat there with my head on the table simply receiving a true blessing from my personal Savior. When Bob finished his prayer, it took me a *moment to look up through my pool of tears (literally) that were on the table. I looked at Bob and his eyes were flowing with tears as well, as he admitted to me that he had never felt such an intimate presence through prayer for someone before. God touched me in a profound and personal way that afternoon, and I will never forget the amazing sense of God's presence in my heart as I had that day.*

Has anyone prayed over you? _____

_____

_____

Have they prayed out loud with you and for you?

_____

_____

_____

James 5:16 lets us know that prayer is powerful, "The prayer of a righteous person has great power as it is working." Prayer is powerful. 1 Thessalonians 5:16 is only three words long: "pray without ceasing." God wants us to constantly be in the attitude of prayer. Numerous Bible verses and stories reveal the power and necessity of prayer. However, I want to focus on another aspect of prayer – the gift of prayer.

We need to take time praying for others. Philippians 2:3-4 commands us to think of others, "Do nothing from selfish ambition or conceit, but in humility count others more significant than yourselves. Let each of you look not only to his own interests, but also to the interests of others." We need to be concerned for others. Praying for someone else keeps us balanced and enlarges the purpose and value of our prayer life.

Job's friends didn't always see the big picture and weren't always there for Job, yet he prayed for them. Job 42:10 says, "And the Lord restored the fortunes of Job, when he had prayed for his

---

When Job took his eyes off himself and prayed for his friends, God blessed him.

---

friends. And the Lord gave Job twice as much as he had before." When Job took his eyes off himself and prayed for his friends, God blessed him. Praying for family and friends should be part of our regular routine. Pray with faith, confidence, and expectation.

Finally, we are even told to pray for those who have or are wronging us. We are to pray for those who are our enemies or who treat us as an enemy.

Did someone's name or face pop in your mind?

_____

_____

_____

Pray!

Jesus says in Matthew 5:44, "But I say to you, Love your enemies and pray for those who persecute you." He also said, "Bless those who curse you, pray for those who abuse you" (Luke 6:28). Jesus was radical. He called His followers to be radical. Christianity isn't for sissies. No one can make us mad. We control our emotions and need to take ownership of our reaction. Pray!

We need to say, "I will pray for you." Then pray God's best for them. Later, we should follow up to see what God is doing.

"I WILL PRAY FOR YOU"

_____

_____

_____

_____

_____

16

FAVOR

*G*od continued to do many miraculous and gracious things for my benefit. One was favor among the Guards. We found that most of the guards were very cooperative with all of our meetings and times together. One night we wrote a curriculum for an all-night prayer vigil, which allowed each man involved to pray through most circumstances in their lives at that time, including family, their case, their safety, and their growth in Christ. I stayed up all night in prayer and study and meditation on God's Word (along with many others), and in the morning, the meanest, and least favorite guard among the men knocked on my door. She simply stated, "Are you alright? I read in the log that you had stayed up all night praying. Is everything OK with your*

An all-night prayer vigil.

---

family?" I answered her and she left. My "Bunkie" looked up at me and stated that he had never seen anything like that in the 25 years he had been locked down. He stated that she is the meanest guard with a "chip" on her shoulder the size of a mountain. He had never seen her speak nicely to anyone before. God was doing miraculous things in our midst. Later in that week, the same guard was working while Bob and I were praying in the day room.

She approached us. We were sure that she was going to kick us out or split us up, but she simply asked us for prayer for something she was going through. We prayed for her while she sat on the other side of the glass in the dayroom. God was paving the way for true ministry and answering prayer all over the compound.

Has anyone treated you well that caught you off guard?

_____

_____

_____

Were they a stranger, new acquaintance, or someone you thought didn't like you? _____

_____

_____

In Genesis 39 we find Joseph in prison. He was innocent. He was accused of trying to rape the commander's wife. He got framed and the hierarchy just locked him up. He didn't have a chance. He didn't get a trial. There was no investigation. His life was in

---

God hasn't forgotten you.

---

the "pits", again. God didn't forget him; "But the Lord was with Joseph and showed him steadfast love and gave him favor in the sight of the keeper of the prison" (verse 21). Joseph was going to be blessed by God and man. Joseph didn't have to feel alone. If you too are a prisoner, or feel in the pits of life, remember God can give you favor.

As a baby, Samuel was given up for adoption to a man who ended up being very evil. The man's sons were also bad news. It almost sounds like a man rendition of Cinderella. Samuel stayed focused on God. 1 Samuel 2:26 records, "Now the boy Samuel continued to grow both in stature and in favor with the Lord and also with man." God didn't forget him. God hasn't forgotten you.

Finally, Proverbs 3:3-4 encourages us; "Let not steadfast love and faithfulness forsake you; bind them around your neck; write them on the tablet of your heart. So you will find favor and good success in the sight of God and man." Expressing love and being faithful is the key formula for finding favor with God and man.

God is amazing. He is so powerful. He is in control.

_____

_____

_____

_____

_____

_____

_____

_____

_____

When you can't,
He can.

Hey, thank you so much for your thoughts on Ruth. That is exactly what I am hoping for. I love your thoughts on Jesus not just a the cross redemption, but every step of His life. Amazing. Each step counts. This is what I am looking for — not theological research, but heart felt sincerity. Thank you — it will preach! ☺

17

KNOW GOD, NO FEAR

*O*ne of the best parts of the prison experience was the diverse and amazing people that I was able to meet and encounter. I was in our church service, preaching one Sunday afternoon and a young man came up to me after the service with several questions. He was passionate about his desire to know more about God and His Word, and he had several poignant questions that revealed he was really listening and attempting to grasp all that was spoken of that day. We made arrangements to meet up in the yard later that evening as we couldn't loiter in the room where church had been held. We met every day in the yard as he was in a different unit than me, and we discussed what he had been reading in the Bible, and I was challenging him to give his life over to the Lord. Soon after that, I woke up early on Christmas morning and was very down and depressed thinking of my family waking on Christmas without me. I was spiraling down into a true depression and decided to go for a walk out in the yard. It was a very cold morning and it was snowing so much, that I couldn't see more than 50 feet in front of me. I trudged on in the snow and was sinking deeper into despair. As I walked past the basketball courts, I heard someone behind me and felt a hand on my shoulder before I could see who it was. It was the young man Mick. He was visibly upset and had been crying when I spun around to *talk to him. I informed him that I was pretty down myself and was not going to be very good company. He asked if we could sit down at the tables, and I acquiesced. Through his tear filled eyes and broken voice, he told me that he was being challenged by God to make a drastic change in his life. He asked me if I would be willing to lead him in a prayer to receive Jesus, and give his life fully over to our God. I sat in the thick snowy Christmas morning*

I was a part of God's broader family.

---

and realized that God had placed me in that very spot to minister and be used by Him for the good of the Heavenly Kingdom. I was immediately refreshed and my spirits were boosted as I realized that even though I was apart from my family, I was a part of God's broader family and was being utilized for His glory even in the midst of that darkened day. My family came to visit me later that Christmas day, and we were able to celebrate the day even though I was separated from them. A volunteer pastor baptized Mick about two months later and even though I wasn't scheduled for that service, one of the guards came and called me out of our unit so I could attend. God continued to do miraculous things regularly!

I don't even need to start with a question. We all have bad days, weeks, months, and even years. Psalm 40:1-3 says, "I waited patiently for the Lord; he inclined to me and heard my cry. He drew me up from the pit of destruction, out of the miry bog, and set my feet upon a rock, making my steps secure. He put a new song in my mouth, a song of praise to our God.

Many will see and fear, and put their trust in the Lord." Our tendency is to read these verses and immediately be reminded that God can rescue us. However, I think we need to relate with the writer when he describes where he was: "the pit of destruction, out of the miry bog." Even the great men and women of the Bible had times when they felt life was beating them up.

In Psalm 43:5 the writer is having a discussion with himself: "Why are you cast down, O my soul, and why are you in turmoil within me? Hope in God; for I shall again praise him, my salvation and my God." I think we all have those times when we talk with our self. Why am I so down? Why doesn't anyone love me? Why do I do such dumb things?

Paul found out from experience that often in our lowest times the Lord shines the brightest. 2 Corinthians 12:9 says, "But he said to me, 'My grace is sufficient for you, for my power is made perfect in weakness.' Therefore I will boast all the more gladly of my weaknesses, so that the power of Christ may rest upon me."

Often when we feel defeated it only brings fear for the future. We buy the lie that it will only get worse. We become so apathetic and pessimistic that we think the light at the end of the tunnel is

In our lowest times the Lord shines the brightest.

a train headed our way. Psalm 34:4-5 brings hope: "I sought the Lord, and he answered me and delivered me from all my fears. Those who look to him are radiant, and their faces shall never be ashamed." God can deliver us from our fears.

Know God, No Fear
No God, Know Fear

_____

_____

_____

_____

_____

_____

_____

_____

_____

18

IRON SHARPENING IRON

My friend Mark and I were inseparable. We were always together in the day room or in the yard talking of God and praying together. Our midnight bathroom Bible studies were continuing with many men being ministered to and prayed over. It was a good time of growth and friendship, and one day, Mark's "bunkie" was told that he was "riding out"! This meant that Mark was going to be in need of a new roommate. One of the guards approached Mark and asked him if he would like it if I was moved into his room so we could spend even more time together. When Mark told me the news, we were both overjoyed. We spent most of the "count times" reading scripture aloud and then praying together as the Lord was leading. We were discussing our families and praying for our loved ones multiple times a day. It was a glorious time of spiritual growth and blessing. We started

---

It was a glorious time of spiritual growth and blessing.

---

making necklaces through the craft room and were selling them so we could send money home or purchase needed items for different men as they had need. It was the true church in action and I was privileged to be a small part of it. Mark was a recent convert, and

I was a recent "reconvert"! We were feeding each other in ways that could only have been orchestrated by God and His wonderful Word. We would have deep thoughts, and bounce them off each other and my spiritual growth was happening on a daily (sometimes hourly) basis. God had blessed me with so many great men and experiences that I was finally able to admit that I was still His child, and God still had a plan for my life there and after. Mark was baptized shortly after that. The guard that called me out to Mick's service repeated the favor by coming to get me for Mark's as well. I was so overwhelmed with joy and emotion watching Mark being dipped into the water, that I knew that God was present in the most real way in that place that was supposed to be awful!

Who is your best friend(s)? _____

_____

_____

Are you a better person because of them? _____

_____

_____

Are they better because of you? _____

_____

_____

God created us with the need for others. You may feel you are better as a loner, but actually we need one another. Hebrews 10:24 says, "And let us consider how to stir up one another to love and good works." We need each other for encouragement. This can allow for accountability and teamwork.

1 Samuel 23:16 brings some depth to the topic: "And Jonathan, Saul's son, rose and went to David at Horesh, and strengthened his hand in God." Basically, it sounds like Jonathan encouraged David. However, it is deeper than just that. Jonathan was King Saul's son. He was the expected and natural choice as the next King of Israel. Yet, he knew David had been anointed by Samuel and was God's choice. Jonathan humbled himself, stepped away from any entitlement as king in waiting, and encouraged David. He and David built each other up.

The Book of Proverbs gives such practical insight: "Oil and perfume make the heart glad, and the sweetness of a friend comes from his earnest counsel" (27:9). Accountability, encouragement, and now counsel are seen as great advantages of having a positive friend.

The last benefit to see here is growth or improvement. Proverbs 27:17 says, "Iron sharpens iron, and one man sharpens another." When needed, we can fine-tune each other. Constructive criticism and directed confrontation can help bring us back in line or take us to a new level.

Accountability, encouragement, and counsel are great advantages of having a positive friend.

Do you feel alone? Do you think there is no one around you? Paul knew the feeling: "At my first defense no one came to stand by me, but all deserted me. May it not be charged against them!" (2 Timothy 4:16). Paul was going through a difficult time and he was alone. However, he knew God hadn't moved: "But the Lord stood by me and strengthened me..." (verse 17). God is right there with you, but His design is for us to have another believer by your side.

Pray for someone you can build and who will do the same for you. Pray, look, and expect God to send someone.

_____

_____

_____

_____

_____

_____

_____

_____

IRON SHARPENING IRON

Hey Bud,

First christmas without my mom, yet I can't imagine what this has been like for you. All I can say is I am praying. I jog daily (5-7 days a week) now and have for 5 weeks. This is an excellent time for prayer.

This Sunday I preach at the chinese church from 1 Thess 5:16-18 (will of God). I feel this passage is an excellent New Year's resolution for anyone.

I have my theme for Benakel speaking. There is a quote that says the difference between a strong christian and a weak christian is 3 words: And then some!

message 1 - Intro
message 2 - God gave eternal life "And then some" abundant life
message 3 - our giving to God - ritual or "And then some"
message 4 - our relationship to one another - Random acts of
      kindness = "And then some"

I am excited about these messages
and challenged to live them.
Somehow I hope God
is even more real to you now.
Strive to enjoy the slower pace

I'm praying for you
with hopeful expectation…
to see the Lord's
faithfulness, goodness,
and abundance
satisfy every need
you are trusting Him to meet.

the "time out" and find Him new.
And then please write me and
share your thoughts and heart. I
want to learn through this, too.

Your friend,

"Be strong and take heart, all you who hope in the Lord."
PSALM 31:24 NIV

Although in prison, he prayed and
fasted for me one whole day.

IRON SHARPENING IRON

19

MY TURN

*A*ll was going well in the unit and at the prayer tables on the yard. Men were being ministered to, accepting Christ, and growing in their love for the Lord. Bob and I were quite a team! I couldn't imagine the prison experience without him. One morning he came out to the prayer table with a heavy heart and tears in his eyes. He simply looked at all of us and said; "I'm riding out right after lunch." I was dumbfounded! I couldn't believe my ears! My first thought was that God would never leave me here alone at these tables without Bob. We spent the last hour of our time together praying for Bob's safety and asking God to pave the way for him at the new facility. A prisoner is never told in advance where they are being transferred. So we simply prayed that God would lead the way for Bob, prepare hearts and men for him to team with in the church, and to minister to at his new prayer table ministry. The next morning I came out to the prayer table alone and concerned that I was not ready or prepared to handle the responsibility on my own. The table quickly filled with men in need and God showed us, once again, that He was the provider and the sovereign God. It was a time of blessing and power, and we all spent time thanking God for Bob's leadership in our lives. Many of the men prayed for me to take on the role as table leader. I felt like Elisha when Elijah simply told him it was *his time to take the reins. I wasn't nearly as equipped as Elisha, but God was gracious and paved the way for continued ministry*

I came out to the prayer table alone.

---

and prayer. I sorely missed my friend and mentor. Soon we were able to write each other and minister to each other through the post. God once again showed His amazing grace and mercy and never left any of us in an abandoned state, even though we didn't always recognize it.

Who has had the biggest impact on your life? _____

_____

_____

Elijah had a time in his life where he thought he was the only man in the world who was faithful to God. He was lonely and depressed. God told him there were 7,000 faithful men in Israel. He didn't need to feel alone and hopeless. He moved forward. On his way, he saw Elisha. 1 Kings 19:19-21 says, "So he departed from there and found Elisha the son of Shaphat, who was plowing with twelve yoke of oxen in front of him, and he was with the twelfth. Elijah passed by him and cast his cloak upon him. And he left the oxen and ran after Elijah and said, 'Let me kiss my father and my mother, and then I will follow you.' And he said to him, 'Go back again, for what have I done to you?' And he returned from following him and took the yoke of oxen and sacrificed them and boiled their flesh with the yokes of the oxen and gave it to the people, and they ate. Then he arose and went after Elijah and assisted him." Elijah threw his cloak on Elisha. It was a cultural way of saying that he would mentor and guide Elisha. They ministered together until Elijah was taken away in a chariot of fire (2 Kings 2). Elisha was left behind to continue the work. It has been noted that Elisha ended up doing twice as many miracles as Elijah. Not everything is recorded, but it still shows Elisha continuing on. It was his time. He took on the challenge. He acted.

Paul and Timothy had a similar relationship. Paul had been the lead man. He had started several churches and was frequently traveling. He relied on other men to keep the work going as he left for another opportunity. Timothy was a young man he trusted. However, Timothy didn't always feel ready or up for the challenge. Paul writes him saying, "Let no one despise you for your youth, but set the believers an example in speech, in conduct, in love, in faith, in purity" (1 Timothy 4:12). Timothy probably used his age as an excuse. Paul still believed in him and challenged him to be the role model for younger and older individuals. In 2 Timothy

---

He took on the challenge.

1:7 Paul had to further remind Timothy, "For God gave us a spirit not of fear but of power and love and self-control." Fear is not from God. God is known for power, love, and self-control.

Luke 6:40 says, "A disciple is not above his teacher, but everyone when he is fully trained will be like his teacher." We need to be developing the next generation. We need to work on creating our replacement.

Also, we need to thank the person (or people) who has impacted our life. We need to continue the process and build up someone else.

Are you intentionally investing in someone else's life?

MY TURN

20

CURSE OR BLESSING?

*M*y new friend Mick, who came to know Jesus on Christmas, began to spend every possible moment he could with me in the yard. He was so eager to learn and was writing down dozens of questions about the Bible each day. We were able to get away to walk or sit and talk about the Lord and His Word. He was always sharing his new found faith with anyone one that he would cross paths with. It was truly amazing to see how God was transforming him and using him to further the kingdom. One day he brought this young man to me that was really bitter and angry and was convinced that God was horrible if He existed at all. We began talking of God, and the young man immediately began mocking and speaking obscenities about "a so-called God of Love!" I asked him why he was so adamant about hating God, and he went on to explain his horrible childhood. His mother would sell herself each night in their apartment and then began selling him in the same way. My heart was bursting for this young man, and I was standing there perplexed as to what I could possibly say to a young man that had gone through so many atrocities at such an early age. How do I explain the love of God to someone that believed that it was God's fault that he went through all those terrible things? While he spoke, Mick was standing behind me with his hand on my shoulder praying quietly *and asking God to give me the right words and wisdom for this difficult situation. Immediately, Psalm 139 came into my mind. I began to talk to this young man about how God uniquely created him, and even knit him together in his mother's womb. I simply shared that God didn't "do" those things to him, but perhaps God allowed those things to happen. God, in His infinite wisdom and*

God uniquely created you, and even knit you together in your mother's womb.

---

love for him, knew him so well, that He wanted him in this place at this time with that mindset. It was the only way that the young man would be prepared to receive the deep and amazing love that God has for him "right now!" I was still standing in a state of apprehension because I didn't know if I was able to minister to this young man in those circumstances. The next event was one of the most amazing that I have ever seen. The young man dropped to his knees and through tears of past torture and renewed joy gave his life to Jesus right then and there! His prayer was one of surrender, repentance, and a true desire to know and love the One True God! God was orchestrating amazing things and continued to offer countless opportunities to us, simply because we were available. We weren't any more prepared than most. We were simply praying constantly and making ourselves available to being ministers for the Most High God!

Do people know you care about them? _____

_____

_____

Authentic sympathy can be a timely gift. Hurting for and with someone else can exhaust us but may be the only instrument the person needs to be able to move forward. When hurting with someone, scripture can give the needed direction. The young man in this prison situation was broken inside and God used someone caring and His own Word (the Bible) to mend him.

Psalm 139 can be broken into four sections. Verses 1-4 explains that God is omniscient (He knows everything):
"O Lord, you have searched me and known me! You know when I sit down and when I rise up; you discern my thoughts from afar. You search out my path and my lying down and are acquainted with all my ways. Even before a word is on my tongue, behold, O Lord, you know it altogether. You hem me in, behind and before, and lay your hand upon me. Such knowledge is too wonderful for me; it is high; I cannot attain it."

God knows everything. He knows our past, present, and future. He knows what we can and can't handle. He allows things to happen, knowing they will draw us to Him. These horrible times actually might be a blessing giving us strength, purpose, and direction for the future.

The next six verses remind us that God is everywhere (omnipresent):
"Where shall I go from your Spirit? Or where shall I flee from your presence? If I ascend to heaven, you are there! If I make my bed in Sheol, you are there! If I take the wings of the morning and dwell in the uttermost parts of the sea, even there your hand shall lead me, and your right hand shall hold me. If I say, 'Surely the darkness shall cover me, and the light about me be night,' even the darkness is not dark to you; the night is bright as the day, for darkness is as light with you."

God is always around. He is never more than a prayer away. Hebrews 13:5 tells Christians that God has said, "I will never leave you nor forsake you." It is such a comfort to know we never are alone. God is there.

Psalm 139 goes on to say that God is all-powerful (omnipotent): "For you formed my inward parts; you knitted me together in my mother's womb. I praise you, for I am fearfully and wonderfully made. Wonderful are your works; my soul knows it very well. My frame was not hidden from you, when I was being made in secret, intricately woven in the depths of the earth. Your eyes saw my unformed substance; in your book were written, every one of them, the days that were formed for me, when as yet there was none of them. How precious to me are your thoughts, O God! How vast is the sum of them! If I would count them, they are more than the sand. I awake, and I am still with you."

The young man in this prison situation was humbled and exalted to realize that God had personally made him. We are one-of-a-kind, handmade, and patented by God Himself. Our fingerprints are as unique as a bar code. God knows all, is everywhere, is all-powerful, and exemplifies holiness. The last six verses of the chapter emphasize the holiness of God:
"Oh that you would slay the wicked, O God! O men of blood, depart from me! They speak against you with malicious intent; your enemies take your name in vain. Do I not hate those who hate you, O Lord? And do I not loathe those who rise up against you? I hate them with complete hatred; I count them my enemies. Search me, O God, and know my heart! Try me and know my thoughts! And see if there be any grievous way in me, and lead me in the way everlasting!"

God is holy and always does the right thing. John 9:1-3 can be a difficult passage. It says, "As he passed by, he saw a man blind from birth. And his disciples asked him, 'Rabbi, who sinned, this man or his parents, that he was born blind?' Jesus answered, 'It was not that this man sinned, or his parents, but that the works of God might be displayed in him.'" God allowed this man to be

---

We are a one-of-a-kind handmade, and patented by God Himself.

---

born blind. Later, we find out that he was blind for 38 years. That is horrible. However, because of his blindness, he ended up "seeing" Jesus. If he were born "normal", he probably would not have sought Jesus. He would eventually have died not knowing Jesus. He would have died in his sin. He would have ended up in Hell. The "gift" of blindness saved him, probably his family, and maybe many more. God knows all, sees all, controls all, and always does the right thing.

Is something from your past holding you back? _____

_____

_____

Is it possible God allowed something bad to happen to you that could eventually be a blessing?

_____

_____

_____

_____

_____

_____

_____

_____

CURSE OR BLESSING?

21

EXIT STRATEGY

*M*y *"bunkie" Mark and I were in our cell one evening when a guard knocked on the door and said to me, "You're riding out in the morning, pack up!" We sat in silence for quite some time. His silence was because he was not yet prepared to lose his friend and be separated. My silence was the same but with a twist of apprehension for what is in store for me next. We spent the evening together as he helped me pack, and we discussed many things. We were able to share our deep friendship and how deeply meaningful our time had been together. I also was able to spend time in the dayrooms with many other friends and co-ministers for our God. It was a time of sadness and celebration as we reflected on the time we had together for each other and our Lord. In the morning, I walked to the administration building and sat in the visitors' area awaiting on a bus to take me to a new location. My mind started racing and thinking that perhaps I would be reunited with Bob. I was excited at that prospect but soon learned as I boarded the bus, that I was heading for a different facility. Upon entering this new destination in my life, I was immediately challenged with the prospects of ministry. We began a prayer table and found that the atmosphere was very different. The "community" of church wasn't really present there. The mindset of the inmates was quite different than I had experienced. The* *focus in this place was "home". Each man had an exit opportunity and was consumed with the date, and the meeting with the parole board that was to come, or had already occurred and they were waiting on the decision. This was a new challenge for me as I was in that same process and possibility in less than one year. A small group of men gave their lives to the Lord, either through the prayer table or in the day room of the pole barn in which I was assigned.*

The focus in this place was home.

The task at hand was to focus on my own exit strategy, making sure that all the necessary requirements were completed, and also to help disciple and nurture these new men in Christ. It was a blessed time in growth! An amazing occurrence took place as people from my past, many of those who were directly hurt by my sin, were writing and asking to visit me. I met with several old friends and was reunited in ways that I would have thought impossible. I had long given up on the idea that anyone that was in the wake of my disastrous sin would ever find the ability to forgive me and move on. I was so thankful for my wife and children. I was sure that their forgiveness and loyalty to me would be all I could expect or hope for. God was moving in the hearts of many old friends and God continued to show His amazing ability to orchestrate and sovereignly move circumstances for His kingdom, His church, and for me personally.

Inmates need to have an exit strategy to be able to cope again in society. Their plan should involve where they are going, who they will be with, and what they are going to do. However, everyone constantly has to consider his or her exit strategy. Going from high school to college, college to the workforce, single life to married life, being just a couple to having a child, and every other key transition needs a plan. God wants to be part of this plan and wants to help. Proverbs 16:3 says, "Commit your work to the Lord, and your plans will be established." We need to pray for what God wants us to do. He knows what is best. This mindset is repeated in Proverbs 3:6, "In all your ways acknowledge him, and he will make straight your paths." God has a plan for us. We need to seek Him. Finally, Proverbs 15:22 says, "Without counsel plans fail, but with many advisers they succeed." It is wise to seek advice from those we respect. We need friends who will be honest with us. Our exit strategy needs to include faith, family, and friends. We need to make sure that with a move, we quickly get into some kind of Christian fellowship. Hopefully, this will involve our family and friends. We need to make sure we surround ourselves with people that have a positive influence on us and us for them. The "old crowd" is not a good plan. Past behavior is difficult to overcome, especially upon exiting prison, or other transitions in our lives. It is too easy to "pick up where

We need an exit strategy.

we left off". We need to break "old" behavior and move forward with God as the Leader, and Shepherd of all our decisions and behavior!

God is interested in our goals, plans, future, family, friends, occupation, activities, and even our everyday routine.

Make wise choices!

What transition of life are you experiencing? _____

_____

_____

What is your exit strategy?

EXIT STRATEGY

_____

_____

_____

_____

_____

_____

_____

_____

_____

22

"I'M NOT THE MAN I USED TO BE"

*T*he new prison offered new experiences and new atmosphere. One of the biggest changes was the size of the church service. This facility had a real chapel that would seat about 400 people. The Sunday service was in the late afternoon. There was one particular day that I went to the service with a very heavy heart about my family and I was simply overwhelmed because of the constant separation. I was going to see the parole board in less than a month and my natural mind was beginning to betray my faith. I was losing confidence and I was allowing the enemy to infiltrate my way of thinking. I was simply not focused on Jesus; my eyes were straying to the reality of my situation (from a negative perspective). I sat in the service and one of my favorite Michael W. Smith songs was being sung. My mind was being transformed back into true thoughts of what God had brought me out of, and away from over the past couple years (it felt like a lifetime at that moment). It was announced that the volunteer was running late, so the worship time was extended and I was being ministered to through singing and praise of our Lord. When the volunteer speaker arrived, he sat down on the steps below the pulpit and put his face in his hands. He began by stating; "I'm not worthy to be here today and speaking in front of all you men. Each time I come here I feel like all of you are more qualified to be up here than I *am." His heart was heavy and he was being as real as anyone I had seen from the preaching position. He stated that he stopped his car about two miles from the prison and sat there on the side of the road debating whether he should continue or turn around and go home. He said that he was there for about five minutes when he finally turned his thoughts toward God and asked God for guidance. After a few minutes in prayer, he decided that he couldn't "let us down", and that he had to fulfill his responsibility to us. His message was a simple one that had the most impact on me of any message that I had ever heard before. While the praise time helped me to begin to focus on God's goodness again, I was still looking at all my own failures and was sitting in that chapel in fear and devastation that day. The man started off by stating;*

I am not the man I want to be.

"I'm not the man I'm supposed to be"! I don't measure up to God and His Word, and I feel as if I'm a failure all the time. He spoke a little more on that part of his message and then continued on with his second point. "I'm not the man I want to be"! He continued with how he looks around at others and sees a quality about their lives and actions, and he knows that he doesn't measure up. Then he stated that when he was sitting in his car wondering if he should continue to the prison to speak or if he should turn around and go home when God gave him an epiphany. He said that the last thing he wants to share with us is something that allowed him to continue here, and that maybe we are sitting out in the audience and need to hear the same message. He simply stated his third point and I was so overwhelmed with God's love and God's voice, that I was sure that man was there only for me that day. He stated his third point; one thing that he had come to realize is that "I'm not the man I used to be"! God was speaking directly to my soul! God's grace helped me to realize that true change had occurred

inside this shell of a man. I had sinned, I had betrayed many, I had failed my God, my family, my friends, and my church, but I am not that man anymore! God's grace had allowed true repentance and true forgiveness. I could look up into heaven with confidence knowing that God had done a good work in me. God had helped me to see the truth of my failure, and God had allowed me to move past my own sin and shame into right relationship with Him, my wife, my children, my friends, and His church! It was the most dramatic realization of my life. "He who began a good work in me will be faithful to fulfill it." It was the true miracle of the Gospel and the reality of the work of Jesus Christ on the cross. The blood of Jesus was not only available to bring us to salvation; it is available to wash us clean on a daily and moment-by-moment basis! My strength was renewed, my mind was renewed, and I could walk with a true understanding that the work of Jesus on the cross was perfect and complete for me and in me!

Do you think you are the person you are supposed to be?

_____

_____

_____

Are you the person you want to be? _____

_____

_____

Have you changed or has your past held you back?

_____

_____

_____

Labels are dangerous. We can change and often the label hasn't.

Not only is it hard for others to see us differently, but it may also be hard for us to feel, notice, or even try to create a difference. Your location doesn't need to define who you are – prison, office without a window, low-income housing, athletic bench, second

Jesus Christ brings new life.

chair, community college, and even "in a van down by the river." We need to be content where we are while constantly trying to grow. We need to be ready for the next transition, position, and location. Life consists of change and it is important we are ready and respond correctly.

Also, your past doesn't need to define you. Jesus Christ brings new life. 2 Corinthians 5:17 says, "Therefore, if anyone is in Christ, he is a new creation. The old has passed away; behold, the new has come."

Are you in Christ? _____

Are you a follower of Jesus? _____

Have you given your life to Him? _____

If so, you are "a new creation".

It is time to do two things:

1. Put off the old self.

Colossians 3:9 says, "Do not lie to one another, seeing that you have put off the old self with its practices." Our old lifestyle of lying, cheating, stealing, selfishness, anger, bitterness, disrespect, thinking evil, and just outright sin needs to be peeled off and thrown into the dirty clothes. Hebrews 12:1 uses the analogy of a runner: "Therefore, since we are surrounded by so great a cloud of witnesses, let us also lay aside every weight, and sin which clings so closely, and let us run with endurance the race that is set before us." Sin holds us back; it keeps us down. Forgiveness in Jesus Christ brings hope. Ephesians 4:22 repeats this deliberate action in saying, "Put off your old self, which belongs to your former manner of life and is corrupt through deceitful desires." Verse 24 gives the other step: "And to put on the new self, created after the likeness of God in true righteousness and holiness."

2. Put on the new self.

We need to put on the new self. Romans 6:4 says, "We were buried therefore with him by baptism into death, in order that, just as Christ was raised from the dead by the glory of the Father, we too might walk in newness of life." We are new people, a new creation, and have newness of life. John 1:12-13 takes the image to another level: "But to all who did receive him, who believed in his name, he gave the right to become children of God, who were born, not of blood nor of the will of the flesh nor of the will of man, but of God." We were born of the world, but now are a child of God. Our ultimate label has changed. The labels of our location and our past that society, friends, and even family have placed on us have changed.

Christians are "a new creation" walking in "newness of life" as "children of God."

I believe in the miracles of God, for only He can turn:
    A MESS into a MESSAGE
    A TEST into a TESTIMONY
    A TRIAL into a TRIUMPH
    A VICTIM into VICTORIOUS

_____

_____

_____

_____

_____

_____

_____

_____

_____

"I'M NOT THE MAN I USED TO BE"

Happy Easter! I am praying for April 21st! I look forward to some very positive news. The next phase of life will be difficult. Freedom does not automatically come outside some bars. Jesus brings real freedom. I know you are already free. Accept Jesus' forgiveness daily and live confidently free. You are awesome and truly a friend to me. Your new setting might be God's way of preparing you for change. The church is very similar to your setting. The only difference is new & old. You are with "new, struggling, wavering christians".

the church is full of "old ...."
I expect it from new christians - older
christians becomes shameful.

I need your prayer for my Thursday
college class. God is doing something. In my
weakness He is strong! I have been sick the
last 5 days and was sick for
class 1. I haven't missed
a class and fought through
it. I that satan is
attacking and God is winning.

> May the Lord
> smile on you
> in a special way this Easter,
> and may He bless you
> with His love always.

After class 1, Brian, a student, said he went
home and opened the Bible for the first time
in his life and read til 5:00 AM. PTL!!
Jenifer said she wanted to know more about
God. Pray for this class of 16 adults.
God is doing something huge inspite of me.

Love ya bro,

127

"I'M NOT THE MAN I USED TO BE"

23

HONEST PRAYER

I *had come to a place of peace and trust in God. He had shown Himself so faithful in so many ways, that I knew I was in His hands in every way! I was so in touch with God through time in prayer and time in His Word that I was certain that no matter what the outcome of my parole board hearing, I knew that it was God's sovereign hand that was in control. I would like to qualify that statement with an understanding that I had learned in my in-depth time with God in prison. We are often taught that if we have faith that means that we aren't allowed to have emotion or the ability to desire a certain outcome. I was often told that if I truly had faith, then I was not allowed to think negatively or question the possible outcomes. I was simply to accept (blindly) what that outcome was and not question whether it was for my benefit or not. I really wanted to be paroled and allowed to go home to be reunited with my family. I was receiving all kinds of "opinions" and counsel as to how I was allowed to think while in prayer for my upcoming parole board meeting. One group was stating that I had to "claim" my parole and that would force God's hand in making it happen. Another group was stating that I needed to simply ask for "God's will", and I was not allowed to attempt to superimpose my will on God's plan. It was becoming a confusing time in my life as I was simply trying to lay myself in God's hands, and all these confusing opinions were infiltrating my peace. God led me to the time when Jesus was in the garden of Gethsemane, and His prayer was one of request and His desire to face His trials in a certain manner. Jesus asked His Heavenly Father if He could "remove this cup." We know that Jesus never violated any of God's commands and certainly never committed any sin. I learned that when we are in times of struggle and times of desperation, God allows us to bring all our thoughts and burdens to His throne in prayer. I desired to go home, but I also knew that God had been faithful with my renewed life in that time in prison. I was resolved to go or stay, but my strong desire was to go home. I spent hours a day in prayer asking God to grant me the ability to go home and be with my family again. I was convinced that it was honoring to God to bring my true thoughts and desires before Him. We often get caught up with the idea that we can play games with God or play on words in prayer to manipulate a situation for our good. God doesn't want our games; He sees through our manipulation.*

I had come to a place of peace and trust in God.

There isn't some "magic" formula to say in prayer to force God's hand. God wants your true heart; He wants you to lay yourself before Him with complete openness and a pure heart. Jesus asked for His desire but quickly realized that He was on this earth for a specific purpose and aligned Himself perfectly with the will of the Father when He said; "not My will, but Thy will be done!"

Do you view God as watching over people waiting for someone to mess up so He can "zap" them? _____

_____

_____

Do you think God wants to bless you (Matthew 6:3-4 says, "But when you give to the needy, do not let your left hand know what your right hand is doing, 4 so that your giving may be in secret. And your Father who sees in secret will reward you)?

_____

_____

_____

God is described as a loving Father. This concept may be very foreign to you. We start the Lord's Prayer referring to God as our Father, who art in Heaven. Psalm 68:5-6 describes God as, "Father of the fatherless and protector of widows is God in his holy habitation. God settles the solitary in a home; he leads out the prisoners to prosperity, but the rebellious dwell in a parched land." God, as Father, cares about orphans, widows, the lonely, and prisoners. God created love and is willing to shower it on us. He wants us to talk with Him. He loves us.

Psalm 37:4-5 says, "Delight yourself in the Lord, and he will give you the desires of your heart. Commit your way to the Lord; trust in him, and he will act." Follow Christ and watch your dreams put on shoes and begin to walk. Please capture the last three words of these verses "he will act."

An interesting story is recorded in Luke 18:1-8:
"And he told them a parable to the effect that they ought always to pray and not lose heart. He said, 'In a certain city there was a judge who neither feared God nor respected man. And there was a widow in that city who kept coming to him and saying, 'Give me justice against my adversary.' For a while he refused, but afterward he said to himself, 'Though I neither fear God nor respect man, yet because this widow keeps bothering me, I will

give her justice, so that she will not beat me down by her continual coming.'" And the Lord said, 'Hear what the unrighteous judge

God is described as a loving Father.

says. And will not God give justice to his elect, who cry to him day and night? Will he delay long over them? I tell you, he will give justice to them speedily. Nevertheless, when the Son of Man comes, will he find faith on earth?'"

A lot of discussions can go into analyzing this story; however, we shouldn't lose sight of the first sentence –"they ought always to pray and not lose heart." God does want us praying "the desires of our heart". He wants us to keep on keeping on in prayer.

"The Christian life is not a constant high. I have my moments of deep discouragement. I have to go to God in prayer with tears in my eyes, and say, 'O God, forgive me,' or 'Help me'" (Billy Graham). Reverend Graham has reached millions of people and still let God know what he wanted and even asked God to help him.

Finally, Charles Spurgeon advises, "If you believe in prayer at all, expect God to hear you. If you do not expect, you will not have. God will not hear you unless you believe He will hear you; but if you believe He will, He will be as good as your faith."

_____

_____

_____

_____

_____

_____

24

GOOD NEWS

---

*T*he morning had finally arrived! I was going to see the parole board for a hearing to determine if I would be released on my first possible "outdate." I had fasted for a day and had prayed for most of the night asking God to pave the way for the hearing, and to grant me wisdom and confidence. When I was led into the office, it was a small room with a desk where the parole board member was seated, and two other chairs, one of which was occupied by my wife. I was happier to see her there than I was at the idea of the hearing. The discussion began, and I was asked all kinds of questions about my crime, my time, and my relationships outside of prison. The board member then directed some questions to my wife, and she was amazing, loving, and totally on point with her answers and responses. At one point while I was speaking, I stated that I was possibly the worst criminal in this prison. I felt that I had a greater responsibility as I was a Christian and even was working in ministry at my church. That comment made the board member stop, look up, and take off his glasses. It also made my wife gasp (quietly) and all eyes were on me to elaborate. I did. The hearing continued for about 15 minutes more. The board member simply said that he would make his recommendation to the board, and I would hear from them in three to four weeks. I was completely sure that God was *directing all thoughts and decisions in that room that day, and I was truly resolved for any decision because I knew it was directly from God's sovereign hand! We left that room, and my wife went into the visitor's area for a visit since she was already there. We discussed how each of us thought the hearing went, and she wasn't real pleased with my comment about being the worst in the place. The next several weeks were filled with prayer, writing letters to friends and family, and time in the yard at the prayer table and in discipleship. I would like to say that my faith was rock solid, and I was completely at peace with God's plan, but the reality is that I was keeping extremely busy doing "anything" and "everything" to not allow my mind to retrace all the discussion in that hearing. I must admit that I was anxious and hopeful at the same time, while trying my best to keep my focus on serving God, prayer, and Bible study. That wasn't always the case. Many times I found myself*

I stated that I was possibly the worst criminal in this prison.

---

in the yard walking and worrying, and over-thinking the process and praying with a sense of desperation. God was always faithful in giving me encouragement from others, the right passage about worry and casting my cares to Him. The day came after three weeks of waiting, and the unit counselor called me to his office over the paging system. Two friends took my hands and said a quick prayer and I was off to the office to hear about the next phase in my life. Basically, the two options were: release and under parole supervision in the world, or "flop", which would mean another two years behind bars before I would receive another parole hearing. I entered the counselor's office and he simply looked up and said, "I have good news and bad news, which first?" I, of course, picked the good news. He said, "You received your parole!" I was so overjoyed instantly that I said to him, "That said, there can't be any bad news!" He then stated, "You have a three-year parole instead of two." That didn't even phase me. I was going home and God had brought me through the most difficult of times and had proven Himself faithful in countless and immeasurable ways to this undeserving man!

Do you remember a time when someone told you they had bad news and good news for you? _____

_____

_____

Which do you typically want to hear first, the bad news or the good news? _____

_____

_____

Bad news and good news are part of life. The Bible clearly presents our predicament. There is bad news. First, the Bible says we have all sinned, "for all have sinned and fall short of the glory of God" (Romans 3:23). I think if we were honest with our self, we would have to admit we have sinned. My friend was quite bold when he said, "I was possibly the worst criminal in this prison." Not

Jesus died for us.

only have we sinned, but also it brings a consequence. Romans 6:23 says, "For the wages of sin is death, but the free gift of God is eternal life in Christ Jesus our Lord." Sin brought death. On our own, we are in trouble. We have sinned, we are lost, and this leads to death, even Hell.

Fortunately, The Bible also offers good news. Romans 5:8 says, "But God shows his love for us in that while we were still sinners, Christ died for us." This verse acknowledges us as sinners but still presents good news. Jesus died for us. The Bible also explains our part in benefiting from this good news. Ephesians 2:8-9 says, "For by grace you have been saved through faith. And this is not your own doing; it is the gift of God, not a result of works, so that no one may boast." The good news includes our salvation. It comes by faith in Jesus.

Are you a follower of Jesus Christ? _____

_____

_____

If not, why? _____

_____

_____

If so, what are you doing with it? _____

_____

_____

I trust through this book, those who are in prison and even those who are "free" but trapped by life, will find the hope, value, purpose, and meaning that can only come through the Lord Jesus Christ.

John 8:36 says, "So if the Son sets you free, you will be free indeed."

_____

_____

_____

_____

GOOD NEWS

I had to go out an get a cares for this one. I am so pumped. Again, God is so good. I hadn't thought about all the strikes against you and just figured "you did your time" and now come home. But this really is a miracle. Thank you Jesus. Remember in college our "chin up" ~~PTL~~ PTLA. Mike, I am extremely happy fix you, *your wife* and the kids. Hey, Tom got his MDiv. That is cool!

I guess
you could say
I was happy
to hear
your good news...

*C*ongratulations!

Finish strong!

Love - your friend,

GOOD NEWS

25

HOME SWEET HOME

*T*he day of my release was finally there. My wife picked me up from the prison, and we spent the day together in freedom for the first time in three years. We went to a mall. I must say that it was awesome but also a bit overwhelming, as the noises, smells, and atmosphere was something that I had put out of my mind in defense for quite some time. My parole officer was an amazing person, and I could instantly perceive that he was "on my side" and desired to see me succeed. God was again gracious and faithful in my re-acclimation into society. A great friend was in the process of giving me a job, and another faithful friend gave me employment instantly as I waited for the long-term job. My wife, children, and friends were again a pivotal part of my daily life. I was so thankful and grateful. I got involved in a small church, and to my amazement, a small group of young men and past friends wanted to start up our own version of a "prayer table." We had a weekly Bible study at my house, and God was blessing us. I must say, though, the continual consequences of my crime and sin is an ongoing issue as a "felon." I use discretion and discernment in everything that I do. I don't want to put anyone in a situation that they would feel uncomfortable. The past still has an impact on my family and me on a daily basis, but God continues to bless and pave the way for us to move forward and *serve Him and to live a life of substance and grace. If you are in a place of sin in your life, seek God for forgiveness but also seek out a close friend to confide in and deal with the sin in a proactive way.*

Give your life to Jesus.

Don't let any sin in your life fester and grow. God loves each of us too much to allow us to live a life of deception and sin. He will bring it to the light and the consequences will be real. We are all born "prisoners!" Our prison is a sinful nature. This nature has us in bondage and chains from living a free and blessed life. God sent His only Son Jesus to give us the remedy for this bondage in sin. Trust in Him, give your life to Him, and allow God to bring you into a right relationship, breaking the chains of sin in your life, and you will be blessed and free!

_____
_____
_____
_____
_____
_____
_____
_____
_____

HOME SWEET HOME

"All things work together for good to those who:

① Love God

② called according to His purpose."

I see these Requirements in your life. God is blessing.

The initial information from the parole board is discouraging, but we know God has not forgotten you or your family. He has the best for His children. Less than 1 month sounds amazing. Bro' I am with you!

please pray with me. I
am doing a funeral wed night
for the family of a 7 year old
boy who was killed in a boating

right
on!

accident. Tragic! I am asking
God for wisdom and comfort.
Mike, walk out of prison with your
chin up (Remember PTL. A) you are
a new MAN! Amen and Amen.

Your friend & brother,

EPILOGUE

Where was God through all this? The most important lesson that I learned from all my experiences, trials, failures, and sin was that God was always by my side. God was always faithful! God was always loving, compassionate, caring, and looking out for my best interest. I failed God on so many levels, yet God was always right by my side with His sovereign touch, orchestrating all of my encounters, and preparing the way back into His loving arms in a "right" relationship with Him. I did so many things to fall short of Him. I even gave up on my faith in the darkness of my soul. God never gave up on me! Romans 8:38-39 reads; "For I am convinced that neither death nor life, neither angels nor demons, neither the present nor the future, nor any powers, neither height nor depth, nor anything else in all creation, will be able to separate us from the love of God that is in Christ Jesus our Lord." The list from that verse includes everything that we can think of to separate us from God, yet He has promised us to continue in His love ... "No Matter What!" God has been the mighty composer throughout my entire life. He was mightily active in my life when I felt that I wasn't deserving. We all can conclude that God loves us and has an amazing plan for each of us as we trust in Him. Take the leap of faith and give yourself over to the only Person (Jesus Christ) that can show you such amazing love and purpose.

OUR MISSION

Matthew 28:19-20: *"Go therefore and make disciples of all nations, baptizing them in the name of the Father and of the Son and of the Holy Spirit, teaching them to observe all that I have commanded you. And behold, I am with you always, to the end of the age."*

REACH

At The River Church, you will often hear the phrase, "we don't go to church, we are the Church." We believe that as God's people, our primary purpose and goal is to go out and make disciples of Jesus Christ. We encourage you to reach the world in your local communities.

GATHER

Weekend Gatherings at The River Church are all about Jesus, through singing, giving, serving, baptizing, taking the Lord's Supper, and participating in messages that are all about Jesus and bringing glory to Him. We know that when followers of Christ gather together in unity, it's not only a refresher it's bringing life-change.

GROW

Our Growth Communities are designed to mirror the early church in Acts as having "all things in common." They are smaller collections of believers who spend time together studying the word, knowing and caring for one another relationally, and learning to increase their commitment to Christ by holding one another accountable.

The River Church
8393 E. Holly Rd. Holly, MI 48442
theriverchurch.cc • info@theriverchurch.cc

BOOKS BY DR. RANDY T. JOHNSON

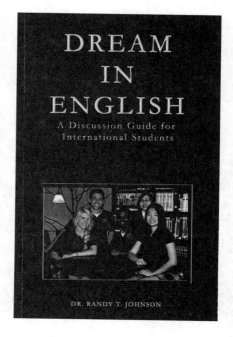